CHEW ON THIS

FIFTY-TWO INSPIRATIONAL POINTS TO PONDER

* * * * * * *

GARY BROCK AND KELLY BROCK TUCK

garybrock85@gmail.com

First Edition

ISBN:978-0-578-42762-1
Library of Congress Control Number: 2018967670

Garcia Publishing Company Garciapubco.com

GPC GARCIA
PUBLISHING
COMPANY

We help families preserve
their unique stories.

* * * * * * *

Dedication

To the experiences of life and all that accompanies them.

To Sara Bjorkquist for reading and providing thoughtful input for each story in this collection.

To Ellen Brock for her editing and unwavering support.

* * * * * * *

* * * * * * *

Mountain of Life

* * * * * * *

Week One

I approached the gate of the Mountain of Life to begin my journey. All I could do was stare at the mountain in awe. "Wow," I breathed, "it's very big...and very high."

A gentle pressure squeezed my shoulder, prompting me to glance at my mother, who was smiling at me. "You can do this. You've been talking about making this trek for a long time."

Swallowing hard, I nodded in acknowledgment of her words. The Mountain of Life was a landmark in our part of the state. People near and far came to climb the one hundred miles to the top while journeying through its winding trails and varying terrain; for many it was similar to a rite of passage. I typically enjoyed the challenge of finding solutions to seemingly impossible situations and found myself in a state of cager apprehension since there was no one set trail to the top.

"Remember," my father began, "it's like I have always said, the journey of one thousand miles begins with one step."

My mother added softly, "And no matter how fast or slow the journey is taking, it will always continue one step at a time."

I smiled, absorbing their last bits of advice, and gave them both a big hug. "So, where should I start?" There were several paths at the base of the mountain. One led to the right, the other to the left, one appeared to lead straight up the center...but there were also several narrow paths streaking in different directions in between. My mother stepped backward to stand beside my father.

"At the beginning," they replied in unison.

Drawing in a deep breath, I stepped through the gate, twisted around to return my parents' waves, and took my first step toward the Mountain of Life. After scrutinizing each possible path, I decided to take the path in the middle to begin my trek up the mountain. As I approached the path, I walked over to the rack of shoes placed precariously at the entrance of the trail. The sign above it read, *Please find a pair of shoes in your size. These shoes have been specially designed for your climb of the Mountain of Life.*

All the shoes held within the rack appeared to be of the highest quality, but they were all different; not one pair, even the ones that were the same size, were identical. After selecting a pair in my size, I quickly removed my shoes, placed them on the rack to await my return, and put on the climbing shoes. As I tightly laced them, I glanced around to find that all of the paths contained a shoe rack. Even though they all held various shoes, the racks themselves were all different.

It was finally time to begin. As my feet took the first steps on the wide dirt path, I soon noticed a large wooden sign in between clusters of pine trees not far from the mouth of the trail that was labeled "Education." *Interesting,* I thought to myself, *I didn't know the trails were labeled. It's even more interesting that this is the center trail and it's the Trail of Education.*

While I climbed the mountain, dutifully sticking to the path, I noticed several offshoot trails. I was curious as to where they would lead, but I stayed the course and continued to focus on the path I had chosen. A couple of times, I unintentionally strayed off of my path and into another. It wasn't until after walking several feet, sometimes yards, that I would happen to see a sign that was labeled something other than "Education." I would turn around, get my bearings, retrace my steps, and return to the course of Education.

After several days traveling up the path of Education, I found myself at an impasse. I could go no further. Several large trees — unearthed or knocked down in what appeared to be at the hands of Mother Nature — blocked the path. In order to continue, I climbed over the large tree trunks. Finally pulling myself up and looking over the fallen trees, a pang of dread filled my stomach as I stared down into a very deep ravine just on the other side of the trees.

Okay, I thought to myself as I continued to stare at the ravine, *what should I do now? Let me backtrack...find a different path.* As my feet treaded in reverse, I decided to mark my steps as a reference point in an attempt to escape the feeling of being lost. For some reason, walking backward actually gave me a little comfort. Maybe the old adage, "hindsight is twenty-twenty" was deep in the back of my mind.

I soon came to the last crossroads before the impasse and immediately froze. One led to the left, the other to the right. *Which one should I take? Which will get me to the top of the mountain? My gaze lifted to the treetops. Well, I don't have any dice to throw or a coin to toss, and it's not like I can draw straws with myself...* My lips pursed. *Okay, both of the entry ways seem to be fairly well defined which means people before me have gone both ways.* My gaze searched for something, anything that would give me some sense of direction. I threw my head up toward the sky and prayed, "God, please give me direction!"

All of a sudden from the left, I heard a bird that distinctly called, "Bob White!" My head whipped around to see a quail flying from its perch on a branch.

"Thank you, Lord," I breathed in relief as I headed to the path on the left. Before I traveled too far, I decided to make a little mound of pinecones beside the entrance just in case there was some kind of maze configuration to the trek. *I don't want to have to be airlifted off this mountain because I keep going around and around in circles and never make it to the top!* As I continued, I noticed the name of this path was "Career." *Wow,* my head shook slightly, *this path is really hilly... Up and down and winding around. This is not exactly a straight forward seeming path, but from the strain in my legs I am certain I'm actually headed up the mountain. That's good because it means I'm making progress.*

As I continued up the Career path, I suddenly came to a fork in the road. *Here we go again,* my brow furrowed. *Which one do I choose?* I walked forward into each one to survey the terrain; the one to the left was rockier than any other paths I had traveled down earlier but was wider, more open, and the path to the right seemed to become more densely populated with trees and shrubs several feet in. After internally debating the pros and cons of traveling each path, I chose the one to the left and continued my journey albeit much slower. While climbing ever so higher on steeper terrain, I also had to navigate around rocks both small and large. This path was labeled "Family," with the name actually chiseled in large stone on the left side about a football field's length inside of the path entrance.

The Family path proved to be extremely strenuous and pushed me more physically than I had been pushed in years. During my sojourn up the path, I was tempted on several occasions to exit as alternate paths appeared to the right or left. However, each time my gaze wandered longingly to the exit paths I told myself, *Hang with it...you can do it.* I knew I was climbing higher and higher, and my labored breathing also signaled that the air was becoming thinner. What I found very interesting was that as I climbed to the top of one hill, I soon discovered there were many more hills to climb.

After I skinned my knee and hand on a jagged rock, I decided to take the very next exit I came to in order to prevent any more bodily harm. In my tiredness, I seemed to be getting a little careless. *And you don't need to be careless when climbing rocks up a mountain.* This new path, marked "God," took a very hard right turn. The further I traveled the more goose bumps dotted my skin. All the Spanish moss hanging from the trees and the haze of fog resting underneath the spindled branches gave it a spooky feel. This was really slow going, and I felt as if I was feeling my way in the dark. Unsettled, I turned off of it and onto another path as soon as the opportunity arose.

My new path was brighter and more open. It was so much clearer that I could actually see the blue sky for the first time in...well... awhile. This path didn't wind nearly as much as the last few and was actually going straight up. After climbing for several feet, I realized I hadn't seen a name for this path and walked for an hour or so before I finally came upon it: "Fellowship and Service." Soon the path led to another crossroads. I could choose to continue by passing through a cavern to the left or a cavern to the right. As I stepped closer to scrutinize, I noticed with curiosity that these caverns were actually marked with signs at the entrance: "Retirement" on the left and "Semi-Retirement" on the right.

After a few moments of thought, I decided to take the "Semi-Retirement" cavern, which led me to a path that transformed almost vertical with foot holes to help with the climb. *Not much longer,* I told myself. *You're getting really close to the top!* About halfway up the climb a new sign caught my eye. When my brain registered the word written boldly on the wood, I froze.

Death.

My heart was pounding furiously against my chest. I glanced up to see that I had in fact reached the halfway point before staring down to see where I had come from. Almost acting out of instinct, my body began to back down out of the Semi-Retirement cavern to enter the Retirement cavern instead. The death sign swirled around my brain as my feet and hands worked tirelessly in sync. Ever so gingerly, I descended to ground zero of the ascent upward. Leaving Semi- Retirement, I stepped into the Retirement cavern and, just like the first cavern, it led me to a path that was very close to vertical with foot holes to help with the climb.

When I reached about the halfway point, I noticed a sign just a few feet above my current position. I could not read it from my current vantage point, but curiously strained to make out the words. A growing sense of dread began to form in the pit of my stomach, and after a couple more feet upward my heart skipped a beat.

Death.

I swallowed against the rising knot in my throat. *What do I do? I can't just turn back now. Not after all that I've endured and accomplished. I sighed. If both of these trails are called the exact same thing, they probably converged at some point along the climb without me realizing it, I have no other option but to continue onward and upward.*

Taking a deep breath, I continued to climb until I finally reached a little berm and pushed myself over. Pulling myself up, I smiled in exhaustion. I had reached the top of the mountain! A swell of pride threatened to burst through my chest. *Wow!* I beamed. *What an exhilarating experience! I made it! This is incredible! I'm so proud of myself! I did it*! I beamed. *I actually did it! I climbed the Mountain of Life!* The week of climbing had been much more than I'd ever imagined. I really couldn't put into words the satisfaction that filled me entirely from having completed the arduous climb.

As I strolled around the top of the mountain, I was taken by its overwhelming beauty, but more so by the expanse of what it overlooked. I gazed out from the top of the mountain to the valley below. My eyes widened. It was unbelievable. *Wow, the mountain is really, really wide.* As I took in the view, I allowed myself to fully absorb my journey; I was exhausted both physically and mentally...and, after a moment of reflection, I came to realize I was emotionally exhausted as well. Taking on the Mountain of Life was a big deal. When I decided to make the climb, I wasn't positive I could actually do it, particularly when one of the requirements was that it had to be climbed *alone.*

As I continued to explore, my eyes soon landed on a monument in the center of the mountain's top that displayed a large bronze plaque. *I'm so tired of climbing,* my shoulders slumped as I headed over to the monument to take the several steps up to the plaque.

"Congratulations!" it read. "You have successfully climbed the Mountain of Life. You are now standing on the 'Mount of Tranquility.' Please put on the special goggles in front of you and walk around the top of the mountain. Look over the side as you walk around the top. If you remember, you put on special hiking shoes when you began your journey. These shoes have a special sensor embedded within them, marking your path up the mountain. As you walk around the top of the mountain, please take some time to view your path up the mountain."

Intrigue and excitement surged through me, replacing the extreme tiredness of my feet, and I quickly put the goggles on before hurrying to walk around the Mount of Tranquility to survey my journey. *Wow,* my eyebrows shot to my forehead, *what a path! There are ups and downs, zigs and zags, straight lines, curves and angles... One thing is for sure, there are no straight lines.* I lifted the goggles away from my eyes to view the natural mountainside, all the while shaking my head. *Just, wow.*

Securing the goggles once more, I surveyed my journey up the Mountain of Life and mused on just how rambling it was. *I sure would hate to have to try and map that out to replicate. There's no way I could get it right.* I removed the goggles, reflecting on all the paths that I had chosen, all the while attempting to remember *why* I had chosen them.

It's interesting that a lot of paths you take, you really don't know where they'll lead. There were some paths I liked, some I didn't, and some I'd even backed out of. But I never knew where any of them would take me, especially the ones I took on a whim. Very interesting. As I returned the goggles back to the monument, I noticed at the bottom of the plaque was a directive that said, "LIFT HERE."

Lifting up the rubber flap, the corners of my mouth widened in a smile as I read the message. It said, "Always remember...

*   *   *   *   *   *   *

You don't <u>find</u> your path in life,

you <u>create</u> it

*   *   *   *   *   *   *

*   *   *   *   *   *   *

Compliment

*   *   *   *   *   *   *

Week Two

Tossing a glance at the full-length mirror, I check myself out one last time before heading to work. *Thank God for mirrors!* I beam at my reflection as I turn this way and that. *Whoever made this discovery was a genius! The personal mirror must have been one of the first inventions for modern man because most people, just like me, love and need to look at themselves for one reason or another.*

All right, I think to myself, *time to scrutinize. Hair is perfectly curled, make-up and lipstick are on point, matching earrings and necklace set sparkle just enough to compliment my new chic sheath dress! These heels definitely show off my calves. Good purchase, girl.* Spinning around slowly, my eyes wander over every angle for one final check. *Perfect! Not only do I look super good, but I feel good too! Watch out world,* I smiled brightly at myself before turning off the bathroom light, *here I come.*

*   *   *   *   *   *   *

Strutting down the office hall as if it were my own personal catwalk, I beam a little wider as I greet my fellow co-workers with a small wave and a cheerful "good morning!" As I continue to sashay to my office, I'm sure that someone will notice and immediately comment on the beautiful presentation I'd worked tirelessly to assemble this morning... me! But as I approach my office door after passing at least ten people... ten people who'd said nothing more than "good morning," or gave me a slight wave or head nod, I sharply veer to the right and into the restroom.

My eyes scour the room wildly and I sigh in relief. *Good, no one else is in here.* Positioning myself in front of the mirror, my eyes scan my reflection, making sure there's nothing on my face or in my teeth, before checking over my hair and outfit. The woman in the mirror stares back at me in bewilderment.

Girl, you've definitely got it going on today! You look fantastic! Everyone else must need an eye exam because they are not seeing this masterpiece! It's still early in the day...maybe they're all still half asleep. Someone will comment on your look later. Just give it some time.

Mussing my hair slightly, I leave the bathroom and make my way into my office to start the workday.

By the time lunch rolls around, I'd conversed with several more co-workers and attended three different meetings...and not so much a peep or double take to confirm how awesome I look! Sinking into a sullen mood, I decide to treat myself to a tropical smoothie for lunch for a little pick me up.

As I step into the Juice Joint, my eyes widen at the two long lines of people waiting for smoothies. From their looks, I figure it's safe to assume an aerobic exercise class from the gym next door had probably just concluded. *Well,* I sigh, settling in line, *at least there are plenty of people here to notice me.* No one seems to spare me a sideways glance as they continue with their conversations and smoothie selections.

As my gaze wanders, I soon spy Eve, one of my college friends, a person ahead of me in the next line over. "Hey, girl," I say, lightly touching her elbow. "How are you?"

She turns and smiles when she sees me. "Hi, Desiree! Oh, it's so good to see you." She runs her hands over her damp hair self-consciously. "I just got through with a boot camp workout next door, and most of us figured it'd be nice to cool down and recharge with a smoothie."

"Oh, girl," I chuckle, admiring her dedication, "you look like you worked hard and that always looks good!"

She smiles. "Aw, thanks. You're too kind. Hey, let's get lunch soon. I'll give you a call later this afternoon and we can set something up!"

"That sounds great," I reply as she steps forward to place her smoothie order. *Desiree,* I think to myself rhetorically, *you look fabulous.* I blow out a sigh and look up at the menu. *Why, thank you, Eve, that's so nice of you to say...*

After paying for my smoothie and leaving the store, my mind circles with thoughts. *With all those people in there, I sure thought someone would have commented on "all of this"... or at least "some of this," especially since they were in workout clothes and I'm all dolled up. What gives?* For the remainder of the workday, I continue to wait expectantly for just one person to tell me I look nice, to ask me where I'd gotten my dress or jewelry, or to notice my hair. Nothing.

By 4:00, most of my work for the day is done, so my thoughts wander to the act of complimenting others. *A lot of times compliments are hard to come by. But why? Why are we all so stingy with our compliments? We're quick to vocalize what we don't like...why should we hold back our opinions of what we do like? Am I also stingy with compliments?*

Soon it's time to head home. Switching off the light to my office, I speedily step into the hall, and practically run over Rachel. "Oh, gosh, Rachel! I'm so sorry." I bend down to pick up the file folder I'd accidentally knocked out of her arms when we crashed together. "I was preoccupied with my own thoughts and just wasn't even paying attention."

She smiles understandingly. "It's no problem, Desiree!" she replies, accepting the file folder from my hand. "You have a great night, and I'll see you tomorrow."

Just as I'm turning to leave, I happen to notice her outfit. She's wearing a turquoise wrap dress I'd never seen her in before. It really compliments her hair and complexion. "Your dress is beautiful, by the way! You look so pretty in it. Is it new?"

Rachel beams. "Yes, it is! Thank you so much! You know, this is going to sound silly, but I've been hoping all day that someone would notice...and you did, so thanks!" She takes a step back to continue her earlier stride. "Well, I'd better get back to it so I can get out of here shortly. See you tomorrow!"

While I walk out of the building and toward my car, I realize that I feel just as good in this moment as I had just before I left my house this morning. Even though I hadn't received a compliment, I'd made both Eve and Rachel smile by giving them one. I learned something today that I need to remember for every day, and that is...

*   *   *   *   *   *   *

When you feel in need of a compliment, give one to someone else.

*   *   *   *   *   *   *

* * * * * * *

Old Dog

* * * * * * *

Week Three

I stepped in the gym and quickly headed to the locker room to change for my midday workout, as I have for the past thirty years. Sometime during my late twenties, I realized the solution to my afternoon slump: eat a healthy lunch at my desk and workout during my hour lunch break. Not only did it keep me energized enough so I could be much more productive for the last hurrah of the workday, but my clothes fit better and my wallet became fatter.

After I hurriedly changed into my workout clothes, I made my way through the gym to complete a challenging twenty-minute elliptical workout before finishing my daily exercise routine with a fifteen-minute full body workout utilizing free weights. I glanced around as I stepped on the elliptical.

Workout Unlimited was far from the most luxurious gym I'd ever been a member of, but it was close to my office and served my needs. Its equipment was practically split into thirds – free weights, weight machines, and cardio equipment. The gym was available to members twenty-four hours a day and had attracted a good mix of clients, ranging from teenagers to seniors. I had noticed the older the member, the more they tended to gravitate to the weight machines for their workout session.

As I began my workout, I noticed an older lady striding across the parking lot to enter the gym. I smiled to myself. I had seen her many times over the past six months, and had actually helped her months ago with several of the weight machines when she appeared to be confused on what to do after she sat down on the equipment. It was during that visit she had shared with me that she had been a long time member of the women only gym You Go Girl that had recently closed down.

She had gone on further to explain in slight exasperation, "Their equipment was nothing like this, and I've even wondered if I wasted my time and money at my former gym." She had chuckled. "Just walking in this gym makes me sweat, and that is something I very rarely did even after a thirty minute workout at You Go Girl!"

As she made her way through the doors, I could see her clearly in the mirrors. Even though she was small, she was strong in stature with her shoulders pulled back and head held high. After putting her keys and pocketbook in one of the cubicles, she turned to the gym floor and happened to glance my way. I waved and she returned it with a big smile.

After several minutes, I was breathing hard, deep into my elliptical workout. This particular workout was one of the harder ones I cycled through. Every five minutes, I increased both the resistance and the incline of the machine. My goal was to burn a minimum of four hundred calories within twenty minutes, although I preferred to make it to four hundred and fifty. The sweat dripped steadily off my chin, landing in a growing pool beside and under the elliptical machine, and my breaths were measured but labored.

As usual, I began focusing on anything that would take my mind away from the arduous task at hand. Glancing up at the TV monitors, I soon found nothing playing was of interest. Turning my sights to the window to stare into the parking lot yielded the same result, so my eyes immediately took it upon themselves to survey the gym floor.

All of a sudden, I noticed a white head of hair on the lateral pull down machine. I could see the stack of weights piled on the machine and, unless my eyes deceived me, *five plates* were methodically going up and down. *Hmmm, five plates,* I calculated to myself. *Each plate weighs twelve pounds, so that makes a total of sixty pounds for her!* That was a pretty good amount of weight for a "little old lady."

Glancing back at the monitor to take in the remaining time of my workout, I drew in a deep breath and closed my eyes to focus. *You've got one minute to go,* I told myself encouragingly. *Now is the time to really push it!* After several seconds, my eyes opened to see the white head of hair now at the seated arm curl machine. I once again mentally counted the weighted plates on her machine. *Three plates – wow! That's great! Besides her age, she can't weigh much more than one hundred pounds! Good for her.*

BEEP! BEEP! BEEP!

My workout was complete. The display panel blinked at me, flashing a big *435 calories burned* at me. *Whew! Good work,* I thought to myself, breaths still labored, as I stepped off the elliptical and headed for the clean-up station to get some wipes for the machine. Wiping it down, I looked up to see the little old lady finishing up on the shoulder press machine, only to walk to the bench press machine. While I watched her, she appeared to be a real gym pro as she adjusted the seat, took out the key, and loaded it to the desired weight with no hesitation at all. Impressive.

Throwing the wipe into the trash, I began toward the free weights and could see the little old lady finishing up her workout. She strode by me smiling as she headed toward the cubicle holding her belongings. I couldn't help but notice her shirt, which read, "Your workout is my warm up." I chuckled. I liked this lady.

After finishing my workout and changing back into my work clothes, I began making my way to the front of the gym to head back to work. Walking across the gym to the front door, I saw T.J., one of the gym's personal trainers, at the front desk.

"T.J.," I asked, "do you know the older lady that was just in here working out?"

"Sure," he grinned, "that's Ms. LaVerne. I've been training her for the last five months."

"Man, she's got it going on!" I exclaimed. "I remember about six months ago she couldn't even figure out how to adjust the seats on the weight machines. You've done a great job with her."

"You don't know the half of it," he replied, leaning in closer for emphasis. "She's up to ninety pounds on her dead lift."

"What?!" I gaped. "No way!"

He nodded vigorously. "Oh yeah! She's up to *ninety pounds* and she only weighs one hundred and ten pounds."

"That *is* impressive," I said in awe.

"You know what's even more impressive?" he asked.

"What is that?" I replied.

"She is *eighty years old.*"

"Man," I shook my head in wonder, "I *am* impressed! She's one of my new role models. I certainly want to be able to do that when I'm her age! Six months ago when I helped her with the machines, I actually wondered how long she would be coming around here. I guess she's got some of that 'bull dog tenacity,' if you know what I'm saying." T.J. nodded his head and grinned.

Strolling across the parking lot to my car, I realized that Ms. LaVerne definitely dispelled a popular old wives' tale because she had proven that...

*　　*　　*　　*　　*　　*　　*

No dog is too old to learn new tricks.

*　　*　　*　　*　　*　　*　　*

*   *   *   *   *   *   *

Windshield

*   *   *   *   *   *   *

Week Four

"And now, starting at forward, the 'man with the plan,' a senior from Naismith, Massachusetts... JE-RE-MY. . . WIL-SON!"

The coliseum erupted in screams and applause as Jeremy jogged determinedly to center court, waving appreciatively to the crowd before high-fiving his teammates as they prepared for the first game of the evening in the Final Four of the NCAA college basketball tournament.

All four teams were blessed with immensely talented players, and it was anyone's call who would win. However, all eyes were on Jeremy Wilson. Wilson, coming off a fantastic senior year, was one of the finalists for the College Player of the Year Award and trying his best to land the number one pick in the upcoming NBA Draft. He was also attempting to lead his team, Spaulding State, to its first ever NCAA National Championship of any kind.

The players huddled with their coaches prior to tip off. The combination of nerves, pressure, and the crowd's noisy anticipation of the game caused an electric tension that pulsated through the coliseum, overpowering the last minute words of guidance, direction, and reassurance the coaching staff offered their players.

The players left the bench to congregate at center court to begin the game as the coaches continued to voice last minute instructions. Once everyone had encircled mid court, there was an immediate hush among the crowd. Everyone seemed to hold their breath as the referee tossed the ball up for the tip off.

Instantly, Wilson took a quick jab step on his defender, grabbed the tipped basketball, and, in a flash, dribbled half the length of the court only to soar through the air for a thunderous dunk! As he dropped back down, the noise echoing around the coliseum could've been measured on the Richter Scale. Chanting rang loud and clear, "Bring the house down, Wilson! Bring the house down, Wilson!"

The first points of the game were definitely foreshadowing – it was *all* Jeremy Wilson.

He was unstoppable – shooting from the corner, from the top of the key, turnaround jumpers, scoop shots, half-hook shots, snagging rebounds, lead the fast break. When opposing players tried to double team him, he passed to the open man for easy baskets. It was a remarkable performance. After it was all said and done, Wilson had scored forty points, grabbed eleven rebounds, and handed out ten assists – wow – a triple double in the Final Four.

Jeremy Wilson had absolutely increased his NBA stock with that performance.

Sunday was an easy practice day for both teams that were victorious in their Final Four Games, consisting mostly of a shoot around as the coaches gave each player various points to think about in preparation for the Monday night championship game.

*　　*　　*　　*　　*　　*　　*

The championship game began in an almost identical fashion to Saturday's semi-finals. "And now, starting at forward, the 'man with the plan,' a senior from Naismith, Massachusetts... JE-RE-MY. . .WIL-SON!" As expected, the coliseum erupted in screams and applause as Jeremy jogged determinedly to center court, once again waving appreciatively to the crowd before high-fiving his teammates as they prepared for the final game.

The players huddled with their coaches prior to tip off. The combination of nerves, pressure, and the crowd's noisy anticipation of the game caused an electric tension that pulsated through the coliseum, overpowering the last minute words of guidance, direction, and reassurance the coaching staff offered their players.

The players left the bench to congregate at center court to begin the game as the coaches continued to voice last minute instructions. Once everyone had encircled mid court, there was an immediate hush among the crowd. Everyone seemed to hold their breath as the referee tossed the ball up for the tip off.

Instantly, Wilson took a quick jab step on his defender, scooped up the tipped basketball, and, in a flash, dribbled down the court, drove to the basket, split two defenders, and soared through the air to the basket! Everyone perched on the edge of their seats! This seemed to be the wonderful finale that his performance Saturday had promised.

Clunk!

The only noises in the coliseum that dared to make a sound were the clomp of Wilson's feet as he landed on the court, the gasp of a few members of the crowd, and the bounce of the ball as it ricocheted off the rim of the goal. Wilson's fans were awestruck in disbelief. He had missed the dunk. Silence and murmurs raced across the stands as the ball was retrieved from out of bounds.

Just as the thunderous dunk on Saturday was foreshadowing for Wilson's gameplay, so was the thunderous clunk at the start of the championship game.

Whether he shot from the corner, from the top of the key, in the paint, tried turnaround jumpers, scoop shots, or half-hooks, the basketball seemed one size too large for the goal. Soon, the crowd's cheers of hope transformed into despondent pleas. At one point, Jeremy could be seen walking up and down the bench lifting towels, searching under and behind the bench, before a fan hollered out, "Hey, Jeremy, what are you looking for?"

"My jump shot!" Jeremy hollered back, which prompted a few chuckles from his loyal fans. The entire game was a mirror of the tip off play. Wilson was undoubtedly suffering through the worst game of his college career.

Spaulding State did win the national title, but it was in spite of Jeremy Wilson, not because of Jeremy Wilson, which, fans concluded, was a very hard pill for him to swallow.

After the cutting of the nets by the Spaulding State team, Wilson was called over to be interviewed at courtside. He jogged over, obviously disappointed but still willing to conduct the interview, knowing what question would ultimately come.

"What happened out there tonight, Jeremy?"

Wilson thought for a moment before grinning sadly. "My favorite basketball player, Charles Barkley, said it best. 'I know I'm never as good or bad as one single performance. I've learned not to believe my critics or worshippers.'"

One of Wilson's teammates who was standing near him clapped a supporting hand on his shoulder and interjected quickly, "You know, my father always said it a little differently. He always said to remember...

*   *   *   *   *   *   *

Some days you're the windshield

and some days you're the bug.

*   *   *   *   *   *   *

* * * * * * *

Who Are You

* * * * * * *

Week Five

The weekend retreat led by Guru Garysheema was packed. The guru's promise claimed that by Sunday morning, during the final hours of the retreat, all in attendance would have a completely new perspective regarding the age-old concept of what it meant to discover "who you are."

For a number of years, I'd been searching to discover the secret answer to the eternal question everyone grappled with at some point in their lifetime: *why am I here?* which ultimately led to, *who am I?* The retreat topic caught my eye and caused me to ponder thoughtfully on the message the guru would cover. If I could determine who I really was, maybe I could finally quench my thirst to discover my own life's purpose.

I scraped together enough money to pay the five hundred dollar registration fee, actually "borrowing from Peter to pay Paul," praying the entire time I was not about to waste hard earned money on the latest New Age gobbledy-gook.

Every seat in the large conference hall was filled. Soft murmurs created a light buzz, somewhat heightening the awareness of our common search for truth. I took my seat and skimmed over the complimentary program distributed by the welcome staff in front of the building. There was only an itinerary and meditation practices to "prepare the mind for the message." Soon, the lights flickered on and off to signal the seminar was about to begin. As the buzz faded away, all of a sudden, walking deliberately from the back of the conference room, strode Guru Garysheema down the center aisle to the stage before us.

The guru appeared to be in his seventies but was actually approaching one hundred. Although his build was slight, he was very sturdy in stature. It was hard to tell what his ethnicity was, and, although I was leaning toward Middle Eastern, it really didn't matter. What did matter was the very obvious difference in his demeanor from the rest of us in the room. This was a man who was very comfortable with himself as well as in his own skin. *Of course,* I surmised, *if you're approaching one hundred I would think you should be comfortable in your own skin.*

A loud but respectful clapping rippled through the auditorium as the guru climbed the stairs to sit on the raised stage. "Thank you," he said, silencing the applause before adding quietly. "Come to center... Center yourself."

He closed his eyes and took a deep breath in. After several long seconds, the members of the audience did the same. A deep breath out from the stage signaled the end of the brief meditation. "Good," he said, "let us begin."

The guru gave a brief overview of what could be expected over the weekend and then, to everyone's amazement, announced, "Your registration fee will be returned to you at the conclusion of the conference."

"Did I just hear that correctly?" I leaned over to whisper to the lady beside me. "Did he say our registration fee will be *returned* to us?"

"Yes," she whispered without breaking her gaze from the stage.

"Wow." That meant the conference was *free.*

Guru Garysheema explained, "I have no need for money, but I do know that many times if there is no commitment, in this case measured by monetary exchange, there is no impetus for learning. If each of you were willing to spend five hundred dollars to listen to me speak, you are all most certainly committed to learning. Since I now know you are committed, I am giving your money back to you. Think of it as 'Christmas in April.'"

The guru continued with his overview, beginning with his life's history, and spending the next couple of hours discussing various lessons he had learned over the past century, which included exercise, nutrition, vocations, relationships, travel, and observations. A pin drop could've been heard in the silence of the immense auditorium, partly because he spoke softly, but mostly because what he had to share was enlightening.

Guru Garysheema clapped his hands together. "I hope each of you has a restful night's sleep. We will start fresh tomorrow morning at 9:00 sharp. Good night, my friends." With that, he stood slowly from his seated position and strode off the back exit of the stage.

I slept well that night, although it did take a little while longer than I had hoped to fall asleep. My thoughts were alive with questions as to what I would discover over the course of the weekend.

Saturday morning began just like Friday night; the conference hall was full of buzz and excitement as the lights flickered on and off for Guru Garysheema's entrance. Just like the evening before, the participants respectfully applauded the guru as he made his way to the stage.

"Good morning," he began after we had once again centered ourselves, "I hope your night was restful. We will now begin." He paused before asking thoughtfully, "Who are you?"

The room was silent. The guru waited patiently for at least a full minute before asking once more, "Who are you?"

I noticed everyone was glancing around quickly, just like me, not sure if they should speak or if the question was rhetorical and simply a guide for our focus. We were all waiting for some form of verbal direction.

"Everyone," the guru said softly, "please stand up... Look to the person to your right, look to the person to your left, look at the person in front of you, look at the person behind you. Stretch your hands to the ceiling while raising up on your toes... Good. Now, please be seated."

"We are all here for the same purpose," he began his explanation. "There is no right or wrong answer on the path to understanding. It is a path to be traveled upon. An ancient Chinese proverb reads, 'the journey of 1,000 miles begins with one step,' so please, speak as you feel led and take those steps. All of you, deep breath in..." The sound of synchronized intake of air was powerful. "And release." All confusion seemed to be blown from the room during the exhale as our purpose for the day's seminar was redefined.

He continued, "Now, who are you?"

Answers to the question were called out all over the room. *Teacher, attorney, welder, nurse* – it went on and on until the guru finally nodded. "Very good to all of you who shared, but that is *what* you are, your *profession*. That is what you *do* to *make a living,* that is *not who* you are. So, *who* are you?"

Once again answers flooded the auditorium from all across the room. *Mother, father, brother, sister, daughter, son...* The guru nodded once again. "Hmm, all very good responses... But, that is who you are in *relation to someone else...* I want to know who *you* are. Who are *you?*"

An easy going guy, an encourager, an over achiever, a hustler, a doormat, artistic... Guru Garysheema nodded and replied, "Yes, but that describes aspects of your personality, and, to some degree, informs me of what other people say *about* you, but *does not* tell me *who* you are; it tells me something *about* you. *So, who are you?*"

American, Black, Chinese, Latino, German, Australian... Guru Garysheema smiled. "Good answer, but no, that is your *ethnicity.* Let's try again, *who are you?*"

Male, female, man, woman... The guru nodded his head slightly and said, "Absolutely, but that is your *gender.*" He stood up slowly and clapped his hands together. "Let's break into small groups. Don't be shy, just get with one or two around you and discuss among yourselves *who you think you are.* Remember 'seek and you will find, knock and the door will be opened to you.'"

For the entire next hour, the auditorium was pulsating with lively conversation. All kinds of hypotheses and educated guesses could be heard throughout the groups. It was obvious everyone was intent on solving the ever-persistent question of "who are you?" It had morphed from a mere three words into an intricate riddle.

My group couldn't seem to get past the descriptions that we all used to define ourselves. We thought we were making progress when all of a sudden someone would pipe up and say, "But that describes part of you. It's not an explanation of who you are." Everyone was intrigued as to where Guru Garysheema was leading us. The conference soon broke for lunch and we were asked to return at 2:00.

It took me several minutes to find an open seat when I returned to the auditorium. It seemed as though everyone had the same idea that I had: eat lunch as quickly as possible to find a great seat and take a few minutes to meditate on the question posed by the guru. I ended up finding a seat towards the back of the room, sitting down with about two minutes to spare.

The Saturday afternoon session began just as the others with a flicker of the house lights, the guru walking to the stage, and a few moments to become centered. "Please, everyone," he began, "reach under your seat and bring out what you find."

I reached under my seat in heightened curiosity. There had to be some item, a relic perhaps, used in ancient spiritual rituals. This would surely hold the secret! My fingers wrapped around something soft and springy. As I pulled the object up and inspected it with confusion, I noticed everyone around me was holding the same common household item: a small loofah sponge.

After many quizzical glances were thrown around the room, Guru Garysheema asked, "What do you have in your hand?"

"A sponge," we all replied.

The guru nodded. "Now, everyone, I want you to come on stage, row by row starting with the front, and dip your sponge into this large ceramic vat. Then squeeze it out in the ceramic vat directly beside it. I will demonstrate." He took an identical sponge and demonstrated what he just explained to us in what seemed like one fluid motion. "Please begin."

Row by row we walked up to the stage and dipped our sponges into the vat, then squeezed out the sponge into the vat beside it. I went through the motions slowly and carefully, gazing once at the guru, who nodded in encouragement as I went through the task. Once we had all completed the exercise and returned to our seats, the guru spoke softly. "Very good. What did you squeeze out of your sponge?"

"Water."

The guru nodded his head. "Let us complete the exercise again, just as before, only start with the back row first and work row by row to the front." As the back row began to come up front, the Guru poured a liquid from a cruet into the vat. Row by row we walked up to the stage and dipped our sponges into the vat, then squeezed it into the vat beside it. I went through the motions once again, noting the difference in color and smell that the liquid in the first vat contained.

Once we had all completed the exercise and returned to our seats, the guru spoke softly, "Very good. What did you squeeze out of your sponge?"

"Grape Juice."

The guru smiled and nodded his head. "Let us complete the exercise again, just like last time, but this time we will start with the first row and then the last row, and then the second row, and then the next to the last row, and on and on."

As the first row stood up and started to make their way to the stage, the guru poured a liquid from a different bottle into the vat. Row by row, we walked up to the stage and dipped our sponges into the vat, then squeezed out the sponges into the vat beside it. I went through the motions once again, noting the difference in color and smell that the liquid in the first vat contained.

Once we had all completed the exercise and returned to our seats, the guru spoke softly, "Very good. Now, what did you squeeze out of your sponge?"

"Vinegar."

"Purple vinegar!" someone called out to specify from the other side of the room, prompting a few chuckles from the audience.

Guru Garysheema smiled and nodded his head. "Our seminar is complete for today. Please, everyone, tonight, think about our morning questions and our afternoon exercises – ponder on the question 'who are you?' Tomorrow we will answer the question that all seek the answer to. Have a good evening, and I hope everyone sleeps well. We will begin tomorrow morning promptly at 9:00."

Having tossed and turned all night in an attempt to solve the riddle the guru had posed, the Sunday morning session came too early. As I sat down in the auditorium, I noticed several others with bleary eyes, puffy from lack of a restful sleep. The session began just like all of the other sessions. The crowd buzzed with anticipation, soon the lights flickered, Guru Garysheema strode to the stage, and we took a brief moment to center ourselves. He bowed as he continued to stand before us, making no movement to sit down as he had during the previous sessions.

He began softly, "I hope everyone slept well. Did everyone meditate on our sessions from yesterday?"

"Yes," rang clear through the auditorium.

"Then tell me, my friends...*who are you?*

A grin pulled at my lips. I knew the answer to this question, and apparently everyone else did too. "A sponge," we all responded. "We are sponges."

The guru beamed and clapped his hands together softly. "Friends, you have learned so much. You have taken 999 steps on your journey of 1,000 miles, but you still have *one more step.*"

He sat down. "My friends, *you* are not sponges, but...your eyes, your ears, your mouth, your skin transmits everything to your brain. Your *brain* is a sponge – it soaks up *everything* around you. So, keeping this in mind, I ask you one more time... *Who are you?*"

The room was silent as everyone soaked in the revelation Guru Garysheema spoke. My mind was racing as I suddenly felt more awake than I have ever felt in my life. I raised my hand slowly and the guru motioned for me to speak. As my face stretched into a wide smile, I opened my mouth and said...

*   *   *   *   *   *   *

We are what we continuously fill ourselves with.

*   *   *   *   *   *   *

*   *   *   *   *   *   *

Choices

*   *   *   *   *   *   *

Week Six

Frankie and Freddie Fly spent the entire day in exploration. They found the sweetness of blooming flowers and helped pollinate others as they flew through the garden. They found some fresh dog poop to land on and laid some eggs to ensure a future generation of bug- eyed, winged creatures. They flew in the cracked window of a parked car and found an old French fry to spit on just for fun. Everywhere they flew seemed to hold some new territory for them to explore.

However, their favorite discovery was an opened two-car garage of a brick house. The garage door had been disabled, allowing them to fly in and out, up and down, and all around with ease. While inside the garage, they raced from wall to wall and from corner to corner. To their delight, Frankie and Freddie also found a food bowl for the dog who napped on the cool concrete floor. They helped themselves to an afternoon snack by munching on the leftover food and immediately took a dip in the water bowl resting beside it. The flies decided they would definitely visit the "resort" again...and bring some friends to show off their discovery.

As soon as the sun had soaked up all the dew, they returned to the garage with several flying friends trailing close behind. Frankie and Freddie led races from one wall to the other and from one corner to the next. Just as before, the flies flew high and low, to and fro.

It just so happened that very close to the front right corner of the garage was the start of a new home for Samantha the spider. Samantha had recently moved into the garage from one of the bushes planted outside of the garage. She knew it was almost time for her home to be pruned, not to mention the outdoor temperature was on the rise, so she decided to relocate to a cooler, safer location.

Samantha was just beginning to spin the support strands for her new home when, all of a sudden, a burst of wind flew by her, knocking her off course. She needed all eight of her legs to keep from falling to the hard ground below. Shaking her head to gather her senses, Samantha once again began to spin the sturdy support strands. Just as before, a blast of wind blew past her. She could see that a stream of flies had torn her line.

After collecting herself, Samantha decided to crawl back into the farthest corner and watch the races from a safe distance. Finally after about an hour or so, the flies grew tired of their games and left the garage. Without the risk of being interrupted again, Samantha spun her support strands.

The next day, Frankie, Freddie, and their friends returned to their new hang out and began their aerodynamic games. Closer and closer they flew to Samantha's staked-out homestead. Suddenly, with a burst of speed, they flew through her house strands, although the flies didn't notice what they were flying through. Samantha merely watched from her high corner on the wall. Just as before, after an hour or so of fun, the flies flew home.

Day after day, Frankie and Freddie flew over to the garage to play, race, and see what other mysteries the garage held. Some days the whole crew came with Frankie and Freddie, and some days it was just Frankie and Freddie. And, day after day, the flies flew through Samantha's strands, which, day after day, were beginning to take the desired shape of her dwelling - a web.

The flies flew with reckless abandon without noticing that each day they were breaking through more and more strands. In fact, they really hadn't even noticed the strands at all! Each time the flies went through Samantha's strands, she patiently rewove them before adding more.

One day as they flew through, Frankie thought he felt a gentle tug. He rested on the wall as Freddie soon landed beside him. "Did you feel anything when you flew through that corner just a second ago?" Frankie asked.

"No," replied Freddie, "smooth as always."

Frankie's wings buzzed in frustration. "I really think I felt something when I flew through. It was like something was tugging on me."

Freddie glanced at the corner. "I don't see anything. It's all in your mind." He laughed. "Oh, or maybe this is a haunted garage! Was a ghost trying to get you?"

"Whatever." Frankie shook his head and flew from the wall. The flies cut their afternoon short and flew on home.

The next day, Frankie, Freddie, and their friends met up to decide where they would hang out for the day. After tossing around several ideas, they decided to head over to the new "in spot"— the garage. As the flies began their assault on the air space of the garage, they assembled in single file order and flew around the top of the garage to graze each of the four corners.

Frankie led the way and, after flying through the front right corner, he was positive this time that he had been *slowed down*. Glancing back over his wings, he didn't see anything, but he knew it wasn't his imagination. He landed on the wall and waited for the others. All of the flies flew through the same spot with Freddie bringing up the rear. They joined Frankie on the wall, and, just like the day before, he mentioned that he felt a little grab, a little pull, as he went through the right corner.

None of the other flies noticed anything and wondered if Frankie was coming down with something. Once again, Freddie shook his head at his best buddy. "You are being way too sensitive. Lighten up!"

Frankie listened to his friends and nodded to pacify them, but he knew he felt something...and he didn't like that feeling one bit. Something about it just wasn't right.

Samantha methodically spun her silk. Her house was almost complete.

Several days later, Frankie and Freddie were hanging out when Freddie said, "Let's go over to the garage and see if anything is going on."

"No, Freddie," Frankie began, wings fluttering as he remembered the mysterious tug of his body, "I don't think I want to go. Not today or any day. I've had enough of that place."

"Oh, come on, Frankie," Freddie pleaded. "There is nothing going on here. Let's go just one more time."

Frankie shook his head. "Man, I'm just not feeling it."

Freddie shrugged. "Suit yourself, but I'm going. I'll see you later."

Freddie made the short flight to the garage, and up and down and round and round he flew. He landed on the leftover food in the pet bowl, skimmed the water bowl, then took off for the 360 degrees flight to graze the four corners.

Freddie flew through one, through two, through three corners and then into the fourth corner, which was located in the front right hand corner of the garage. Suddenly, he was stopped in midair.

He couldn't move!

What's going on? Freddie thought frantically. His heart was beating, his wings were vibrating, but he was going *nowhere*. The more he struggled to fly, the more tangled he became. Soon, there was a new movement bouncing Freddie's cage. He glanced up in dread to see eight legs and eight big black eyes heading his way.

Several days later and after an extensive search, Frankie and his friends flew to the garage in a desperate last attempt to find Freddie. After searching around the garage for a few minutes, they finally spotted a clump of web on the garage floor. Someone must have been cleaning up cobwebs. After closer examination, the flies were aghast!

To Frankie's horror, he spied a broken wing and a foot sticking out from the tangled cobweb and knew immediately it was his best buddy Freddie. The flies were deeply saddened. After trying in vain to drag the fallen web out of the garage, they flew to tell the queen what they had discovered.

After the queen listened to the story, she nodded her head slowly and said, "Boys, always remember...

* * * * * * *

Make good choices,

for the chains of choices are too

light to be felt

until they are too heavy to be broken.

* * * * * * *

*   *   *   *   *   *   *

Colors

*   *   *   *   *   *   *

Week Seven

It was a particularly cold Saturday afternoon and Stella was restlessly bopping around in search of something to do. She played outside earlier that morning, but the north wind had blown in fiercely around lunch time. Stella had bundled up to play on the swing set, but after the biting breeze threatened to knock her over with its icy blasts, she quickly decided to spend the day inside surrounded by warmth.

"Mommy!" Stella called out to her mother as she hung her jacket on her special peg on the coat rack. "Let's play a game!"

"Oh, that sounds like fun," her mother began, smoothing Stella's hair slightly as she stepped around her and out of the kitchen, "but I can't play right now, sweetie. I have to vacuum the house and unload the dishwasher."

"I can help!" Stella fell into step beside her mother as she retrieved the vacuum from the hall closet.

"Okay, well how about if you take all the dishes out of the dishwasher and stack them on the counter while I vacuum," her mother replied. "When I get through, we will put them up in the cabinets together."

Stella skipped to the kitchen and carefully unloaded the dishwasher while her mother began vacuuming. Once she'd stacked all the dishes on the counter, she sat on the freshly swept linoleum and picked at a loose string hanging from the dishtowel draped over the oven door handle to wait for her mother.

After a few moments, Stella heard the roar of the vacuum cleaner hush, and she eagerly popped up in anticipation. When

Mother stepped into the kitchen, she clapped her hands together. "Great job! We can get this done quickly if we work together. Hand me each stack and I will put them in the cabinet."

"Can I put them in too?" Stella asked.

"How about you push one of the kitchen chairs over here, climb up in it, and *you* put the plates in the cabinet. Then you can put the silverware in the drawer and I will get everything else."

"Yay!" Stella exclaimed and threw her arms in the air before scampering toward the kitchen table.

It must be a pretty boring afternoon if putting up dishes can pump up a seven-year-old, her mother thought as she watched Stella from the corner of her eye. Stella beamed at her while sliding the chair up to the counter, and her mother quickly corrected her errant thinking as a huge smile brightened her face. *No, she's excited to help.*

It took no time at all to finish unloading the dishwasher, so Stella's mother rinsed the lunch dishes and handed them to Stella to load into the dishwasher. Of course, loading the dishwasher was haphazard with the exceptions of the silverware, which magically all went into one slot in the designated holder. Once they were finished, Stella pushed the door shut and clapped to herself for a job well done, the sight of which elicited another warm smile across her mother's face.

She knelt down to give Stella a big hug. "Thank you for your patience and the hard work. You are such a big helper! Do you still want to play?"

"Yes!" Stella pulled out of the embrace to grab her mother's hand and pulled her in the direction of the den. "Let's color, Mommy!"

"All right. You get the new coloring book and I will get the new box of crayons!"

Stella ran to her shelf in the den to retrieve the coloring book while her mother opened the arts and crafts drawer in the kitchen and pulled out the new box of crayons. After getting situated at the kitchen table, Stella flipped through the pages of the coloring book until she reached a pretty mountain scene overlooking rolling hills that led down to a valley with a stream running through it. To complete the scene, eagles flew through clouds wafting over the landscape.

Mother unwrapped the box of crayons and handed them to Stella. She quickly opened the box...only to stare down with scrunched eyebrows of disbelief. "All of the crayons are green!" She withdrew crayon after crayon, and even though the crayon wrapper read a different color, blue, red, purple, black, all of the crayons themselves were in fact *green*.

"This box must have made it past quality control," Mother sighed.

"What's that?" Stella asked, staring down disapprovingly at the pile of green on the table.

"Oh, that's the person that makes sure everything is correct before something goes to the store to be sold. There is actually an old saying... 'inspect what you expect.' It looks like that didn't happen with this box of crayons." She glanced down at Stella. "Do you want to see what we can do with the green crayons? Even though they are all green, we can practice different shades of the same color."

Try as they might, except for the valley, the green just did not do justice to the sky, the mountain, the sun, the eagles, or the river. The picture was, well, *green*. "This looks bad," Stella said. "I don't like this...it's not fun."

Mother could not disagree. "Go put your coat on. Let's run to the store and get another box of crayons, and we'll color some more in your book when we get back."

"What if we get another box that has only one color?"

Mother stood. "We'll make sure we check the box before we leave the store. We will inspect what we expect."

During the drive to the store, Stella called out from the back seat, "I really like all the different colors. They're all important."

"You're absolutely right," her mother nodded. "Different colors give everything their own uniqueness, identity, and style. I love colors too."

As soon as they stepped foot into the store, Stella pointed in the direction of the arts and crafts aisle. After quickly grabbing a box of crayons, they headed to the checkout lane. Once she had paid for the crayons, Mother handed the box to Stella. "Go ahead and open it to make sure all the colors are in there before we leave the store."

Stella ever so carefully broke the seal and peeked inside the box. To her delight and relief, all of the colors stared back at her from their freshly sharpened points. "Quality control did their job this time."

Mother laughed quietly. "Let's go home and color!"

They soon sat down at the kitchen table to resume their coloring. Stella selected a jungle scene this time, complete with monkeys, snakes, banana trees, tigers, and a sunny sky. The colorful crayons were soon scattered among the many greens on the table and they began to color.

"Mommy," Stella began after she colored the sun a bright yellow, "I think it's neat what color can do. Now I can tell the sky from the ground, and the monkey from the tiger, and the banana trees from the other trees." She reached for a red. "Crayons are different but the same. They are different because of the color, but the same because they are a crayon. I am glad they're different."

Realizing a huge teachable moment was at hand, Mother said thoughtfully, "Crayons are actually a lot like people."

"How?" she asked, not bothering to look up from the snake she was covering with polka-dots.

"Well, even though people are people, just like crayons are crayons, people are also all different colors, just like crayons come in all different colors. We like it that crayons are different colors because they brighten our pictures up, just like we like it that people are different colors because they brighten our world up."

All that could be heard was the quiet movement of the crayons against paper. After a few moments, Stella reached for a pink crayon. "Then why do people fight all the time about what color they are?"

Mother pondered for a moment. "Sweetie, that's a great question. People have been asking the same question for hundreds of years, and I don't have an answer for you." She watched as Stella gave the tiger brilliant stripes of pink and orange. "I do know that we as people need to celebrate our differences and learn to play nicely with each other."

The room fell quiet once more. Since the beginning of time, much wisdom has come from the mouths of babes and this particular time was no different. In the middle of coloring strokes, Stella said softly, "Mommy...

*   *   *   *   *   *   *

Our differences are skin deep,

but our sames are to the bone.

*   *   *   *   *   *   *

* * * * * * *

Prayer

* * * * * * *

Week Eight

Flying out of the community Greenville airport was a delicate balance between convenient and risky. Basically, the airport served as a commuter hub to the regional Charlotte Douglas

International Airport. I have always found it significantly less stressful to fly out of Greenville instead of driving over an hour to fly out of the much larger Raleigh airport, even though there were many instances of Greenville flights, to and from, being postponed or canceled. Knowing this and being a semi-frequent flyer, I always tried to plan for the unexpected.

Today's morning flight should be a snap, I thought on my way to the airport. I would be making the easy one-hour flight to Charlotte in order to attend the highly anticipated Charlotte Hornets basketball game. There was no connection, I had no checked luggage, and there would be no long treks in the concourses across the Charlotte airport. I was one flight away from the game of the season!

As I strolled into the airport my normal thirty minutes before boarding, I glanced up at the flight schedule board. My heart immediately sank as soon as I saw the dreaded word beside my flight number: *delayed. At least,* I thought to myself as I walked to the customer service desk to check in, *I'm not in any kind of time crunch.*

"Do you have any idea why the flight to Charlotte is delayed?" I asked as I was handed my tickets.

"Yes," the check-in clerk nodded, "it's delayed due to heavy thunderstorm activity. At this point we are not exactly sure of the flight's E.T.A. Sorry I can't give you any more detailed information. As we receive updates, we'll update the flight schedule board."

After thanking the clerk, I turned and made my way to the stairs that would take me to the security check line. Once I made it through, the official wait for my flight would begin. *Please God, I silently prayed while my feet trudged up each step, let the storm pass quickly. You know how much I detest waiting.*

While I put my carry-on bag on the conveyer belt, I couldn't help but overhear the conversation of the two guys in front of me. They were also headed to Charlotte for the game, but it was extremely obvious they were pulling for different teams; one was, like me, a Hornets fan while the other, a northern transplant from Boston, was a diehard Celtics fan.

The good-natured insults shot back and forth as they barbed each other about their teams. I grinned to myself, stepping through the metal detector, as the offenses became more animated with added hand gestures to aid the verbal put-downs.

After a few minutes of really good trash talking, and once we had all chosen a seat in the boarding area for the dreaded wait, one of the guys said, "Man, I have been praying all week that Charlotte will kick Boston's tail!"

"That's funny," the other guy replied, "I've been praying the same, except for God to bless the Green Machine to take the Hornets out!"

My head tilted slightly to the side when I realized that these men actually said the word *prayer* with conviction. *Wait a second, I thought. Does God really care about a basketball game? Furthermore, if Boston wins one guy thinks his prayer has been answered, but if Charlotte wins the other guy will say his prayer has been answered.* My mind continued to dissect their dialogue, and I soon pondered the potential prayers of the respective team owners, coaches, and players... *Each side will be praying for an outcome that favors their team, which, of course, would be in direct opposition of the other team's prayer.*

I looked up at the flight schedule board to see if an E.T.A. had posted and sighed. No change. Once again, I made a silent plea. *Please God let the storms pass. I need to get to Charlotte!*

Soon, another conversation met my ears. Two prospective passengers, a man and a woman, sat behind me. The lady was talking to a gentleman that she seemed to know and was telling her companion that she was flying to Charlotte for a job interview. She spoke at lengths about how the job market had been tight in her field and how this was the only opportunity that had become available for her over the last year.

She went on to say that she was so tired of working two part-time jobs and had prayed and prayed that God would help her get this job. She'd made it through the first two rounds of interviews and this was the third and final interview. The final selection was between her and another candidate. I really felt for her and there was no tuning out the stress in her voice. As her friend offered her reassurances, I found myself saying a silent prayer for God to help her to succeed in the interview and land the job.

The coffee I'd been chugging all morning soon caught up with me, and I left my seat for the nearest restroom. As I pushed the door opened and walked into the men's room, I spied from the bathroom mirror a young man standing at the row of sinks. He was obviously in deep prayer as his eyes were closed, his head slightly bowed, and his lips moving silently.

My footstep echoed slightly on the tile and he jumped, obviously startled. Catching his eye as I continued toward the stall, I asked very sincerely, "Is everything okay?"

"I am just so stressed," he replied hastily. "I have this big interview in Charlotte tomorrow morning and the flight is delayed. I've been trying to find a job in my field of study for a year." He turned one of the faucets to splash a bit of water on his face before shaking his head. "I'm behind on my rent and my college loan payment starts next month. I am one of two candidates going for the final interview for this job and I need it so badly." He dried off his hands and headed toward the door. "I'm just praying that God will help me get this job."

Speechless, I nodded before finally mustering a weak, "Good luck with everything." The young man thanked me and walked out. I stood in the middle of the restroom lost in thought. *Wow, that guy and the woman from the boarding area are going for the same job, and it is pretty obvious they both need the job. Each of them is praying that they will be selected for the position, which means they are also praying that the other will not get it, even if it's inadvertent.*

When I left the restroom, I walked over to the flight status board to see if there was an update on the flight coming from Charlotte. *Delayed.* Heading back to my seat, I sent another prayer heavenward. *Please God, let the storm pass so the flight can take off in Charlotte.* Unlocking my phone, I googled "weather in Charlotte, NC," and saw, much to my chagrin, severe thunderstorms forecasted for the entire day.

Despondently, I glanced up at the airport terminal TV and happened to catch a news update about the severe drought conditions in Charlotte - the worst in their recorded history! The report went on to detail how area churches were holding special Saturday prayer services today in hopes that the thunderstorms would stay through the weekend to replenish the depleted water table. I slumped down in my seat a little, in awe of the information I'd just soaked in, and reflected on what I'd been praying for and how selfish it was given what Charlotte was praying for because of what they were dealing with.

As I continued to ponder on the events of the morning I realized, in a moment of clarity, that each of us wanted God to fulfill our *personal* desire. Prayer was revealing itself as self-motivated and self-centered. Prayer, like I had come to know it, was like most things – individual desire that does not necessarily translate into benefit for all.

Maybe, I began thinking, *we have prayer all wrong. Maybe prayer should be more about listening rather than talking. Instead of asking for petitions, maybe it should be listening for direction. This is what it meant in "The Lord's Prayer" when it was taught, "Thy will be done on Earth as it is in Heaven." Heaven is perfection, which eliminates all of our individual, self-centered desires.*

Now more than ever I finally understood the words of Jesus when he prayed to God…

*   *   *   *   *   *   *

Yet not <u>my</u> will, but <u>Thy</u> will be done.

*   *   *   *   *   *   *

* * * * * * *

Reality

* * * * * * *

Week Nine

The other day on my way home from work, I dashed into the neighborhood grocery store, Food Town, to pick up a few items for supper. I briskly strode up and down the aisles, dropping all the necessary ingredients for a delicious lasagna recipe in my basket, all the while praying to make it to the check-out lane before the 5:30 rush. As soon as the cashier handed me the receipt, I made my way to the store exit with bagged groceries and the Food Town basket. I plopped the basket on top of the stack beside the door, and, as if on a whim, left the handles in an upright position.

The next person who needs a basket can just reach out and grab it without breaking their stride, I thought to myself. *That'll save them a couple of seconds, which will be nice especially if they are in as big of a hurry as I am.* A smile slowly spread across my face at my small act of kindness and how it would help the next person coming to shop. As my feet stepped over the threshold of the store exit, sounds of consternation from behind burned my ears.

"What inconsiderate, lazy person left the handles up on the top basket in the stack? Unbelievable! My hands are full! Now I have to put all these bags down so I can fix the handles of this basket so mine can fit in. I don't have time for this! I've got to get home!"

Cringing slightly, I glanced over my shoulder to see a middle age woman struggling to adjust her bags and the basket in her arms before ultimately giving up and dropping her basket with a clatter to the floor. "Oh forget it, the store can handle this. Maybe they should put a sign up telling folks to *put the handles down* when returning a basket to the stack."

She huffed by me and out of the store. My spirits plummeted. What I'd considered to be an act of kindness had actually been an act of aggravation. Bummed, I trudged despondently to my vehicle. As I set the groceries in the back of the Jeep, I realized I'd forgotten to purchase some bread for our "Italian Meal." I spun on my heels and briskly headed back into the store just in time for the 5:30 rush.

After grabbing another basket and filling it with bread and butter, I checked out, grabbed the basket along with my grocery bag, and went to return the basket to the top of the stack. This time, I made sure to push the handles all the way down so as not to cause any more unnecessary struggles to prospective shoppers.

As I was leaving the store, a young mother passed me with a little one in her arms and walked over to get a shopping basket. She shifted the baby from one arm to the other, bent her knees, and bowed her back to lift one handle at a time in order to take the basket out of the stack. Of course, all of the juggling was just what the little one needed to get cranked up.

She bounced the restless baby while finally lifting up the basket and whispered to him in a soothing voice, "You know, for once it would be really nice if someone would leave the handles up on the grocery basket so the next person coming through could grab it and begin shopping without missing a stride. I really don't understand why people can't be more thoughtful. Maybe the store needs to put up a sign telling everyone to give their neighbor a hand and *leave the handles up* for the next person shopping."

My jaw dropped as she walked away. Nothing I did had mattered. I hadn't been helpful at all, and I'd left the handles up and down. All I had wanted to do was be kind and considerate of the next person, but all I ended up being was a hindrance. What was a person to do? I guess it was important to remember...

*   *   *   *   *   *   *

Reality is truly a matter of perspective:

Yours <u>and</u> Theirs.

*   *   *   *   *   *   *

* * * * * * *

God

* * * * * * *

Week Ten

The university's lecture hall for "Religious Studies 101" was crammed wall to wall with students, even though it was not a required course of study or prerequisite for any curriculum. It could be assumed by the quick close out of enrollment and the sheer capacity of the class size, students were mentally calculating, *Religious Studies = Easy A.*

Professor Dogma strode imperiously into the lecture hall, prompting the slouching students to sit straighter in their seats. He proceeded to present a quick overview of the course and instructed the students which website to visit for the syllabus. Explaining his attendance policy, the professor said, "You are all grown and paying for this class. If you want to attend, great, if not, that's your business." A few claps and a solitary whoop echoed through the hall.

Professor Dogma adjusted a few papers in front of him and leaned forward against the podium in the center of the room. "Show of hands— how many of you believe in God?" The majority of the class raised their hands without a second thought. A few hands wavered. The professor's eyes scanned the room. "For those of you that don't believe in God, is it perhaps...because of those that *do?*"

Some of the class laughed and some shifted uncomfortably in their seats. A few eyes widened while others glared harshly at their professor. "This class is titled Religious Studies. We will be studying religion. But before we can continue, we must identify or define what *religion* is. Do any of you know?"

A few mouths opened before promptly shutting and a few hands rose and fell in rhythmic fashion. The sheer size of the classroom intimidated even the boldest of students. The question lingered for a few long seconds before Professor Dogma stepped around the podium and clicked the remote to a projector. *RELIGION* stared back at them in bolded red letters.

"Religion," he started, miming for the class to begin their notetaking, "is defined as the belief in and worship of a superhuman controlling power. Another name, but not the only name, for a superhuman controlling power is... Can someone guess it?

"God?" offered a brave soul from the middle of the crowd.

"Precisely," he continued, clicking to the next slide. "Therefore, in essence, this course could also be titled 'God Studies 101.'" He threw a meaningful glance over his shoulder to the class. "You notice I said *studies* and not *study*. Study being singular and studies being plural... Hmm... And why do you think I used plural instead of singular?" No one dared to venture an answer to the question.

"There are approximately seven billion people in this world that each of us live in," he said. "According to the latest statistics, the number of people that either do not believe in religion or God totals *just less* than one billion. That's one seventh of the *entire population* on Earth. Imagine if every seventh person you met or interacted with on a daily basis did not believe in a higher power." He paused slightly as the students soaked in the statistics. "Before I conclude today's lecture, maybe you will understand why that is."

The class, thoroughly intrigued, intently listened while vigorously scribbling notes as the professor dove headfirst into the initial lecture. His voice was both engaging and entertaining.

"So, we have roughly six billion people that believe in God, a higher power. Of those six billion people, approximately two billion practice the Christian religion, one and one-half billion practice the Muslim religion, one billion practice Hinduism, and all the rest are spread over 4,297 other known religions."

He paused to survey the hall of students. Most were concerned with copying down notes. A few were whispering to each other with wide eyes. Some were gawking at the screen and professor. He waited a few long minutes until everyone was watching him with interest.

"Did you all hear me?" he began again softly. He spoke slowly for emphasis as almost every student sat on the edge of their seat. "There are approximately *4,300 different religions* practiced *right now* on Earth." He paused again to take in their shocked faces. "This basically means there are 4,300 *different* definitions of God because, as we just learned, religion is 'the belief in and worship of a superhuman controlling power.'"

"Even the main religions," he clicked to the next slide, "Christianity, Islam, and Hinduism, have all kinds of different denominations and sects. Beneath the umbrella of Christianity are the Catholics and Protestants, and under the Catholics and the Protestants are *hundreds* of differing denominations with specific doctrines that define religion or define God. Beneath the umbrella of Islam there are the Sunnis and the Shiites, and under each of those main belief systems there are various sects with specific doctrines that define religion or define God. Beneath the umbrella of Hinduism there are Shaivism, Vaishnavism, Shaktism, and Smartism. Each of those belief systems have specific doctrines that define religion or define God."

He returned to the podium. "And that is just the most popular three. There are 4,297 other religions and their subcomponents that define a belief in and worship of a superhuman controlling power." As he searched the crowd of his newest pupils' amazed faces, he mirrored their expressions to momentarily break the serious tone and threw up his hands. "O-M-G, and can I get an *amen?!*"

A mixture of laughter and a very boisterous *amen* rang clear through the entire building. Professor Dogma smiled. "If you do not believe in God, I can certainly understand why. It is probably because of those that believe since there are *thousands and thousands* of ways that we as humans define religion to explain God. Remember, from the beginning of recorded history as far back as documented cave drawings, the human being has always worshipped something greater than itself."

Murmurs and nods of agreement buzzed around the hall. Professor Dogma clicked to the last slide indicating the final minutes of the class. "So, in this initial lecture have I managed to thoroughly confuse you, inform you, infuriate you, or, dare I say, bore you?" He was met with a mixture of expressions, all of which embodied some of the emotions he expressed in his question. He nodded.

"At the conclusion of each semester's first lecture, I always ask a question. Tell me, since there are endless ways that teach how to define God, how do we know which of these ways is right? Or if all of them are right? Or if any of them are right? Each of them proclaims they point the correct way to God. What is one to do? It is after pondering all of these factors that the real question arises. How will you or how do *you* define God?"

The lecture hall was silent as introspection saturated the air. Professor Dogma leaned against the podium, studying each face. Finally, from somewhere in the depths of the lecture hall a still small voice said...

*   *   *   *   *   *   *

Is it not better for God to define you than for you to define God? For as you live your life so shall you define your God.

*   *   *   *   *   *   *

*   *   *   *   *   *   *

Difference

*   *   *   *   *   *   *

Week Eleven

Camping retreats had become a new wrinkle in the corporate team-building phenomena. Purportedly, plucking a bunch of "starched shirts" out of their narrowly defined and controlled business environment and dropping them in the middle of nature for a weekend was designed to build comradery, group decision making, and trust – all necessary skills for successfully managing large corporations and their employees.

The five executives of Rule the World Company, guinea pigs in the "Wilderness Survival" pilot program, were dropped off around 5:30 Friday afternoon at the entrance of the *Who Knows What's Out There?* Camping Grounds and Park. The executives shuffled around as they waited for the retreat to begin, making small talk, surveying the camp ground, and spending their last few precious minutes of freedom with their electronic devices, frantically responding to voicemails, emails, and text messages, before giving them up for the weekend.

Soon, the retreat facilitator, Sarge, a gruff but very fit middle age man, strode up to the group and welcomed them to the camp before tossing each person a black duffel bag. He instructed them to head to the camp bath house and change into the identical t shirts and shorts provided in the bags, and then to pack all their clothes and belongings inside of it.

As the executives trudged to the bath house, he called out, "Remember, no electronic devices whatsoever! No jewelry, no watches, no nothing! Just come back in your new clothes and bring the bags. I'll hang on to them until Sunday afternoon for safe keeping."

Upon returning to the appointed rendezvous spot, Sarge instructed the executives to set up camp. They were confused since there were several cabins clustered around the bath house. As they stared down at the mess of a large tent Sarge was pointing to, he laughed. "What, did you all think you'd come out here for a luxurious weekend? No! Teamwork and collaborative problem solving every step of the way, starting with this tent.

"Directions?" one of the executives inquired timidly.

"Do you mean *instructions?*" Sarge asked. Before anyone could reply, he continued, "Nah, figure it out for yourself. Now, everyone hop to it! No tent, no shelter to sleep under tonight."

Two of the executives inspected the materials in a heap at their feet while the rest turned questioningly to Sarge as if still expecting some initial guidance. Sarge only nodded, crossed his arms, and leaned against a nearby tree, watching as half-hearted attempts transformed into a determined group effort. Sarge noticed quite readily that there were no engineers or outdoorsmen in the bunch, but kept his mouth shut and clapped when they finally managed to rig up a stable tent.

After setting up camp and kindling a scorching fire, everyone began eating franks and beans while Sarge led a discussion on the purpose of the retreat, goals for their company, and how each person's individual success must be in sync with the corporate mission to ensure corporate success. They discussed how each and every individual makes a difference and how each executive must understand that fact or they were doing the company, their fellow employees, and shareholders a disservice.

He reminded them, "A chain is only as strong as its weakest link." Sarge encouraged each executive to take that same message to their respective direct reports explaining that *everyone,* more specifically *anyone,* could make a difference.

On and on Sarge pontificated, driving his point home, and soon the executives' eyes glazed over as they slumped down in front of the fire. "Hey!" barked Sarge, adding volume to his already boisterous voice, intentionally causing the executives to jerk back into the present. "That's enough corporate psychobabble for one night. Who wants to hear some good old fashioned 'deep in the woods' killer animal stories?"

As the fire was stoked and blazed higher, stories filled the smoky air. Tales of psychotic and bloodthirsty bears, wolves, and coyotes. Of wild boars, rabid raccoons, opossums, and bats. Of killer owls, snakes, and lizards. The more fantastical the stories flowed, the stiller the air and trees seemed to become. Eyes widened, jaws clinched, and some of the executives were perched on the edge of their logs while others shrank into themselves.

Suddenly, the fire popped and they all jumped as a yelp pierced the air. Amused at their skittishness, Sarge heaved up a pail full of water. "Lights out. Rest up. You've got many challenges to complete tomorrow. See you bright and early." He tossed the water on the fire, leaving the executives with only star light to guide them to the tent.

They settled into their sleeping bags, murmuring various comments of the first task, what trials they may have to face in the morning, and impressions of their facilitator, and soon tried to drift to sleep. Just as breaths were turning rhythmic and even, a tiny buzz sounded. A few swatted at the air, others smashed pillows against their ears, but the buzzing persisted. Off and on through the night there was a grumble, a sigh, a slap against skin. *Buzz, buzz, buzz* was all they heard. As soon as they began to drift to sleep, back the buzzing came. Not one of the executives could locate the source of annoyance. All they could do was pray it would cease long enough for them to get some sleep.

It didn't.

A bullhorn sounded loud and clear directly in front of the tent, and all the executives moaned in protest. It couldn't be morning. No way! They hadn't slept at all.

"Rise and shine!" Sarge barked exuberantly. As the executives stumbled out of the tent, they were greeted by Sarge's enthusiastic orders to circle around the ashes of the previous night's fire. He passed around protein bars and noticed their drawn and weary facial expressions.

"So," he began, chewing his breakfast slowly, "how was everyone's sleep last night? I slept great!" The air was soon filled with a myriad of complaints as each of the executives grumbled. Sarge leaned forward. "What? Was someone snoring? Did those beans get the best of one of you? Were you cold? Hot? Were those animal stories before bedtime just too much for you? Did you hear some growling, howling, or slithering? Was it the – "

"No!" one of the executives finally interrupted. "It was that incessant buzzing that kept us up all night!"

Sarge's eyes narrowed. "Buzzing? What do you mean buzzing?"

"It was a buzzing noise that would not stop! None of us could find it and it would not stop!"

"So, it was tiny *buzzing* that kept you all up last night. Is that correct?"

"Absolutely!" two of the executives answered in unison.

"Without a doubt."

"It was unbearable!"

"Just the worst.".

Sarge nodded slowly. He finished his protein bar, slapped his knee, and stood up casually. "Well, suits, your retreat is over. You've already learned the most important truth that this entire weekend was designed for. A truth that will make your company as successful as it can possibly be. A truth that you should add to your mission statement and, more importantly, impress on each of your employees."

He searched each one of their confused faces before crossing his arms in front of his chest. A grin stretched wide across his face, and he said...

* * * * * * *

If you ever think you are too small

to make a difference,

try sleeping with a mosquito.

* * * * * * *

* * * * * * *

Flower

* * * * * * *

Week Twelve

Although time had only recently changed to greet the coming winter months, Jim Burpee found himself already weary of the chilly shortened days. Fewer sunlight hours meant less time to spend outside enjoying nature, his favorite place to be after a long day's work. A landscaper at heart, Jim decided to call his green thumbs to action and plant a flower garden in order to lift his spirits.

Around and around his treasured yard he strolled to determine the precise location for his vision to take root. He thoughtfully pondered several factors in his mind as his search continued for the perfect spot. *What location would provide maximum sun exposure to ensure beautiful coloring for the petals? Which areas would allow me to see the blooms as I come and go from home? Surely others would enjoy the beauty of the flowers, so where would be the optimal position to ensure they could be seen from the road?*

After finally selecting an open area in the front side yard and surveying the sculpted shrubbery he'd planted over the years, he decided it would be great to have vibrant bursts of colors from February through November. A smile touched his lips when he realized next year this time he would only have a few months of "gray days" to endure. As he meticulously planned his garden, he consulted his calendar and sketched out a rough diagram. Daffodil and tulip bulbs for late winter and early spring, followed by pansies in mid spring, and finally marigolds and vinca for painting the landscape of late spring, summer, and fall.

Jim could hardly wait. He spent time each evening transforming the open space into a lovely bed waiting to be filled with an assortment of bulbs, seeds, and flowers. Surrounding the newly turned dirt with a beige stone border, Jim stood back and smiled. Soon, brilliantly colored petals would beam at him from their carefully planned abode.

The following Saturday morning, Jim whistled a tune as he made his way down the driveway and began a mile trek to his favorite store, Plant and See Nursery, to buy the bulbs needed to begin his project. Jim enjoyed the sights and sounds all along the way. Once he arrived at the plant nursery, he studied the fact sheets of both the daffodil and tulip bulbs, ultimately settling on a wide assortment of each that held the promise of sunny yellows, bright whites, and a variation of pastels mixed throughout.

During his walk home, Jim gently slung the bag of bulbs over his shoulder. As the bulbs settled, their weight pressed upon a slight tear in the bag, forming a hole large enough for some of the smaller bulbs to escape through. Bulbs dropped intermittently all along the way home; some rolled into dead underbrush, some plopped down in the ditch, some rested next to the trees and bushes along the side of the road, a few settled beside a sign post, and one even rolled up against a rusting fire hydrant.

Once he arrived home eager to begin, he dutifully marked the exact and measured placement of each bulb in the garden. Jim relished the feel of the cool dirt around his hands and fingers as he dug into the barren flowerbed to create a resting place for the first bulb. He retrieved a bulb from the bag and gently plopped it into the hole. Just as he covered the bulb with a blanket of dirt, his wife called from the garage. It was work. There was an emergency and they needed him immediately.

After placing the bag of bulbs on his gardening shelf in the garage, he called his children out to the side yard. He asked them to plant the bulbs while he was away at work and gave them specific instructions on where and how to plant each one. He soon left for the office and the children went back to their Saturday morning.

The bulbs were forgotten.

Later that afternoon, Jim called his oldest child, Jeremy, to ensure that the bulbs were planted. His son assured him that, yes, the bulbs were planted just as they were instructed. Jim thanked him and told his son he would be returning home within the next two to three hours. As Jeremy hung up the phone, he grabbed his brother and sister and they dashed outside to plant the bulbs.

They stared at the empty garden, struggling in vain to remember the very detailed and specific directions their father had left for them. Not wanting to disappoint him, the children quickly planted the bulbs somewhat haphazardly in the garden and immediately raked the topsoil over the bulbs to cover up their planting miscue. When Jim returned home, he smiled in satisfaction. In a few short months, he would be greeted each day by magnificent colors whose faces would brighten the area, smiling for everyone to see.

Jim waited patiently for the short days to lengthen and ultimately for the first glimpse of the flowers growing below the soil to break through the earth.

Soon the green stems began to rise above the soil. Jim observed the garden each day, watching in satisfaction and anticipation, and counted the number of stems, waiting for more and more to appear. He found himself confused over the randomness of the stems pushing through the ground and the miniscule amount that were popping up.

He finally asked his children if they planted all the bulbs where he originally marked them and if they planted all that were in the bag. His children hung their heads slightly and confessed they did not exactly follow Jim's instructions, but that they did plant all of the bulbs. Alas, Jim was greatly disappointed that the number of stems did not come close to matching the number of flowers he was expecting, nor that they were growing in the locations he had so carefully planned.

The bulbs grew their stems larger and longer, soon formed buds, and finally bloomed. What a magnificent sight! The placement had not mattered. The bursts of yellows, whites, and pastels brightened Jim's spirits daily; although there were not as many flowers as he originally planned and they were planted in a random assortment in the ground, their beauty brightened the world with their colorful smiles.

Meanwhile, motorists up and down the road between the Burpee house and Plant and See Nursery could be seen pointing and smiling at intermittent clumps of whites, yellows, and pastels waving along the side of the road, in the ditches, around bushes and trees, and even beside a sign and fire hydrant. Some even left their vehicles to take spontaneous spring photographs using the beauty of the flowers as the backdrop.

No matter the location, no matter the placement, the flowers Jim planted in his yard and that he "planted" from the roadside reached people from all walks of life with the message of Spring and new beginnings. Life may not always go according to the plan you mapped out for yourself, but it is important for you always to...

*　　*　　*　　*　　*　　*　　*

Bloom wherever you are planted.

*　　*　　*　　*　　*　　*　　*

*   *   *   *   *   *   *

Billy and Bobby

*   *   *   *   *   *   *

Week Thirteen

Billy Goat and Bobby Goat were best friends, and they spent almost every day knocking around Farmer McDonald's horse pasture, nibbling at grass, and butting random objects, including each other's heads. Their home, the pasture, was almost five acres and housed a stretch of woods for shade, a barn for the horses, and a trough full of water.

Although there was plenty of space for Billy and Bobby, as well as the horses to roam around in, there was a fence encircling the entire pasture to protect them from getting into any trouble. Typically in the winter, Farmer McDonald threw out hay for feed and filled a couple of pans with grain for the animals. Now that warm weather was fast approaching and nature was rapidly springing up, the farmer only put out hay a couple of times a week since there was now plenty of green to eat.

One very nice spring morning, Billy and Bobby decided to spend their day searching for new territory to graze. As they walked around the pasture looking for new greens to sample, Billy suddenly spied some rich looking grass beside the woods line...right on the other side of the fence.

Billy nudged Bobby, "That looks so good over there. Check it out!"

Bobby gasped as his eyes took in the sight of the tall green grass. The sun shone on it in a way that made the morning dew sparkle. All of a sudden, he noticed that the fence separated them from it. "It looks delicious," he groaned in longing, "but there's no way we can get to it."

"Don't say that," Billy stated, traipsing forward until his face was a mere six inches away from the fence. "I've always heard that 'if there's a will, there's a way.' I'll find a way!" After giving the fence a long hard look, he first made several attempts to simply reach his head over the fence but couldn't stretch far enough to reach the grass.

"Told you so!" Bobby called over in amusement as he stretched out to watch.

"I'm not done yet," Billy replied, slyly looking over his shoulder at Bobby. "I've only just begun." He then decided to shimmy underneath the space between the fence and the ground. He lowered to his front knees and stuck his nose in the free space but, try as he might, he could not make any headway.

"Ready to give up yet?" asked Bobby between mouthfuls of grass.

"Nope," Billy said without bothering to turn around. He took a large step back to survey the situation and his mouth watered as he gazed at the lush green grass *just* on the other side of the fence. All of a sudden, Billy noticed the grid-like pattern the fence had been constructed in. He beamed. He could actually fit his head through the squares that made up the fence!

In one quick motion, Billy leapt forward and stuck his head through one of the lower grids before munching away at the sweet crunchy grass. Bobby was awestruck and immediately trotted over to the fence. "Unbelievable!" he shouted.

Coming up for air, Billy turned his head and grinned at Bobby in triumph. "Mm, mm good!"

Bobby lowered his head. "How exactly did you do that?"

"Pick a hole, then turn your head sideways and stick it through, and waalaah! You will find yourself at a fine banquet hall." He bit off an enormous mouthful of grass, chewed, and swallowed before turning back to Bobby.

Tentatively, Bobby held his breath and carried out Billy's instructions. He soon found himself face first in a palate of fresh greens and...oh, it was even better than he imagined! His eyes fluttered shut as he chomped on the green goodness from the new spring grass, thinking all the while, *It just can't get any better than this!*

All of a sudden they heard Farmer McDonald hollering, "Hey, you two, what are you doing?! Get back in this pasture!"

In the blink of an eye, Billy pulled his head back through the hole and ran on down the fence line away from the farmer's booming voice. Simultaneously, Bobby attempted to pull his head back through. In his haste, he didn't turn his head at the right angle and his horns became stuck in the fence's grid. Try as he might, he could not free himself from the clutches of the fence, and he let out a cry when he received a sharp thump on the rump from the farmer's work boot.

Thrashing around made it no better for Bobby. With his peripheral vision, Bobby could see Billy sprinting to the far end of the pasture. "Hold still, hold still," Farmer McDonald stated as he patted Bobby comfortingly, "let me see what we've got here, Bobby. We'll get you out of there."

He quickly surmised he would have to free Bobby from the other side of the fence. Skillfully climbing over, he grabbed both of Bobby's horns and deftly twisted his head while pushing it back through the fence. As he was freeing Bobby, Farmer McDonald asked, "Bobby, what were you thinking? You've got horns on your head! Of course, you're going to get stuck." As soon as Bobby was free, he took off down the fence line to put as much distance as he possibly could between him and the farmer.

Once Bobby made his escape, Farmer McDonald walked the entire fence line to determine if the problem could happen again. Lush green grass grew thick around the entire perimeter of the pasture. After realizing that the goats, like people, think the grass is greener on the other side, he decided it best to turn on the electricity that surrounded the bottom and top of the pasture fence. After a couple of good shocks, the goats would get the message to stay inside their vast confines and then he could turn it off.

The next day, Billy and Bobby were back to bebopping around the pasture. Bobby had quickly moved past his irritation with Billy for abandoning him to fend for himself against Farmer McDonald. As they walked by the horses, the goats noticed they were feasting on some freshly sprouted maple tree leaves. And, boy, did they look tasty.

Billy glanced at Bobby and said, "Check out Hi Ho Silver and Trigger! They sure are working those maple trees over!"

Bobby chuckled in agreement. "Yeah, seems like they are really chomping at the bit."

Heading toward the fence line, Billy's sights were still set on the trees on the other side of the fence. "It's been a while since I've had any maple tree leaves, and that maple syrup Farmer McDonald puts in our feed is the bomb! As good as that syrup is those leaves have got to be phenomenal." Billy carefully placed his hoofs on the top of the fence, stretched his neck, and began pulling some of the leaves off. "Man," he sighed in satisfaction, "these are *amazing*."

Bobby held back, surveying the situation. Billy once again lifted up off his hind legs, put his front two hoofs on the fence, but this time ripped off a branch of the tree and landed munching on pure maple goodness.

Bobby thought to himself, *Well, if Billy can do it so can I.* He trotted up to the fence and lifted up off on his hind legs to carefully place his two front hoofs on the fence line, just as he'd seen Billy do seconds earlier. He hesitantly pulled a few leaves, hopped back off the fence, and began chewing. He immediately gulped them down, eager for more. How sweet they were! Hopping back up on the top of the fence line, Bobby reached high and far, just like Billy, to snag a branch for himself, but he lost his balance and slipped off. Both of his legs landed directly on top of the electric line.

Zap! Zap! Zap!

Bobby was seeing bright blue stars as he finally fell off the strategically placed electric line and hit the ground. Shaking his head, he looked up to see the line clearly mounted four inches above the top of the fence line. And once again, Billy was nowhere to be found. As soon as the first *zap* sounded, he high tailed it across the pasture as if he was the one that had been shocked.

Watching the scene from a across the pasture, Farmer McDonald hollered, "Bobby, you need to start thinking for yourself because…

*   *   *   *   *   *   *

Imitation can be the greatest form of flattery, but lead to the greatest form of stupidity.

*   *   *   *   *   *   *

*   *   *   *   *   *   *

What Do You See

*   *   *   *   *   *   *

Week Fourteen

It had been great having Joe over to visit for the last several days. We'd instantly clicked the first day of dorm life our freshman year and, even though we'd gone our separate ways after college, had remained the best of friends throughout the years.

Giving Joe a tour of my town and the surrounding areas had been fun since we visited several places that I hadn't been to in years. Our last stop before he returned home would be to the Greenville Museum of Art; it was currently hosting an art exhibit this week featuring the best of the best from the recent North Carolina art competition "Battle of the Brush Strokes."

As we drove through town sipping our coffee and commenting on the ever-changing landscape, we both noticed a heavy middle-aged man, about our age, soaked in sweat and struggling to keep a steady pace as he jogged on the sidewalk. I winced slightly. Both Joe and I had really tried to take care of ourselves through the years and enjoyed all kinds of physical activities, and we also tried to eat relatively healthy.

"Wow!" Joe exclaimed. "Check out that guy over there! He's huffing and puffing so hard it looks like he's about to blow a gasket!" He chuckled slightly. "I believe he's had one to many Krispy Kreme doughnuts, am I right?"

I smiled a little at Joe's amusement. "You know, aging is tough man, particularly if you put on some weight. It's quick to put on and slow to take off."

"As slow as that guy's moving, I don't know if he's really doing anything. I mean, I can walk faster backwards than he's jogging forwards." Joe snickered. "I sure hope he doesn't keel over in the road."

"Come on, man, give the guy a break," I stated, watching the man in the rearview mirror. "At least he's trying."

"If that's what you call it," Joe mumbled, deflated.

"Joe, he's got to start somewhere! Remember my favorite saying, 'the journey of one thousand miles begins with a single step.'"

"Oh yeah," he glanced out the window, "how could I forget..."

We drove on, continuing our conversation about the sights and scenery of Greenville. "I really think you're going to enjoy this exhibit," I said as we came closer to the museum. "I read the review in the newspaper last week, and it is supposed to showcase some of the finest artwork produced by North Carolina artists in years!"

Turning onto the road leading to the museum parking lot, the landscaping on either side of the road immediately caught our attention. The bushes were trimmed and sculpted into different shapes of various sizes. A mixture of squares, rectangles, triangles, circles, octagons, pentagons, trapezoids, and cubes lined the drive.

"Those are really good," Joe breathed, taking out his phone to take a picture. "I'm going to try that idea with my own shrubbery when I get back home."

"Yeah," I agreed with him, "that would add a lot of character to any yard."

As I pulled into an open parking spot, Joe pointed to an oval area of ground covering right in front of the museum entrance. "That is just unbelievable!"

"What?" I inquired, shifting the vehicle into park.

"Are you blind, man?" he asked in disbelief. "They have all of this beautiful shrubbery leading up to the museum, but let the weeds grow up in front of the entrance!"

"Weeds, huh?" I responded, scrutinizing the area to understand his negative outburst.

"Yeah, look at all that clover – weeds, man – I would definitely have to put some serious Round-Up on that stuff to kill it, roots and all." We left the car and headed toward the steps to enter the museum. A sign in the middle of the clover caught my eye. It read, Oxalis – considered a weed in many parts of the United States, *Oxalis is a revered ground cover in many parts of the world.*

"Hey Joe!" I called. "Did you read this sign?"

"Uh huh. Not buying it," came his response as he casually hiked up the stairs.

Walking through the museum was a real treat for us since we were both appreciators of art. We took our time meandering through the exhibition, taking in the beauty of each piece on display. Each exhibit was arranged in order of the individual piece's ranking according to their placement in the "Battle of the Brush Strokes" competition. The judges had consisted of art critics, artistic peers, and the general public giving a really good cross section to vote on appeal, style, technique, and so on.

As we worked our way through the exhibits, Joe and I discussed our anticipation to see the Grand Prize winner located at the end of the last corridor. It had to be nothing short of stunning, as all the works of art we'd seen were fantastic! There had been everything from landscapes to seascapes to portraits and plant life, all the result of the creative genius of each artist who'd meticulously brushed each color onto their canvas.

Finally, we rounded the corner to the focal point of the exhibit: the Grand Prize winning painting of the first annual NC "Battle of the Brushstrokes" competition.

We stepped in the room, and I immediately beamed as my eyes landed on the colorful painting positioned on a polished easel underneath a spotlight in the middle of the floor. The vibrant colors were breathtaking in their arrangement as one seemed to merge into another, creating hues of colors all their own.

"Oh my God!" Joe exclaimed in disgust, much louder than appropriate. Thankfully we were the only ones in the room.

I lightly elbowed his ribs. "Shh, man!" I whispered.

"That is just awful," his nose scrunched and his eyes winced. "What did the painter do, throw a couple of cans of paint on the canvas and run his brush back and forth and up and down? My five year old can do that!" He turned to me in disbelief, motioning toward the painting. "Do *you* call that *art?*"

"It's an abstract. You need to look at the texture, the color, the arrangement. Close your eyes, take a moment, step back, and then open them." I paused. "Taking all that into consideration, *now* what do you see?"

"Uh, something that looks like one of my five year-old's finger paintings," he replied dryly before spinning on his heel. "Come on, let's go. I don't want this painting to ruin the whole exhibit for me."

As we headed out of the museum to the car, I thought about the interactions in regards to the observations Joe and I had experienced all morning, meditating on our conflicting views. Suddenly, I was reminded of a very wise saying told to me long ago...

*   *   *   *   *   *   *

It's not what you look at that matters,

it's what you see.

*   *   *   *   *   *   *

* * * * * * *

The Space In Between

* * * * * * *

Week Fifteen

What we do not see is much more important than what we do see." Guru Garysheema's voice was calm and clear as he began his monthly YouTube lecture for any and all who cared to listen to his wisdom, or dared to challenge their own thoughts, truths, and beliefs. In a very non-confrontational manner, Guru Garysheema forced people to think outside the boxes they and their life experiences had confined themselves to, which made most people uncomfortable. As I liked to elegantly phrase it...the man was artfully skilled at getting in your head!

I began religiously listening to the guru after attending his "Who Are You?" conference, which was personally life changing for me, as his subtle guidance and intense thought provoking questions led me to the understanding that I was the sum of what I filled myself with and, further, that the filling process was all under my control. I had a very sudden awakening to the fact that I'd been filling myself with a lot of junk and not all of it was related to the food I'd been consuming. I returned home anxious to begin filling myself with healthier, positive elements.

Grabbing a pillow from the couch to sit on, I soon perched in front of my laptop, eyes glued to the screen, and with a pen and notebook, I sprawled on the floor. The guru slowly repeated his initial statement. "What we do not see is much more important than what we do see." Guru Garysheema held up a white sheet of paper with a dot in the middle and asked, "What do you see? A dot? Yes, but more importantly a lot of white. How do you see the dot? Well, because of the white space surrounding it. I ask you, is the dot the primary focus? Yes, it is, but only because of the surrounding white space. Without what you do not see, which is the blank space, you cannot see the dot."

"Another example," the guru held up a picture of a pretty home adorned with shrubbery of all types and islands with various ornamental grasses. "What makes the landscaping so striking? Is it the shrubbery? The islands? Or is it the space around the shrubbery and islands, the space without anything growing within, that makes the landscaping come to life? If the entire yard was filled to the brim with these beautiful arrangements, would you be able to notice each one? No. It is the space without that gives the arborvitae its softness, the holly its stiffness, and allows the beautiful colors of the flower petals to pop within the sea of green. I ask you, in this photo is the landscaping the primary focus? Yes, but only because it has been brought to life by the part around it that has no landscaping."

"I love music," Guru Garysheema laced his fingers together, "particularly beautiful symphonies. The way the music flows with purposeful, graceful movement, the emotions the music itself can create, and the story the music can weave without using a single word..." he sighed. "I agree with the great cellist Pablo Casals when he said, 'the most important thing in music is what is not in the notes.' Ah yes, the space between the notes, the space of silence which makes the notes come alive, the space between the notes with no sound makes the sound created by the notes meaningful in the composition. Without the beats of silence there would only be unrecognizable noise."

"In recent times, physicists have discovered the world of Quantum Physics. They have discovered that the atom is not nearly as stable as once hypothesized. In physics, we learn that in an atom there is a nucleus containing a proton and a neutron, which is circled by an electron. Now, based on scientific experimentation performed by the world's most esteemed physicists, on the subatomic level, there is 'free space' between the electrons and the nucleus, and 'free space' between the protons and neutrons. Instead of being static, the sub atomic particles have space in between which allows them to vibrate, creating energy. I ask, is it the subatomic electron, neutron, and proton that are most important for the atom to function, or is it the empty space in between which allows them to move?"

"When you are driving down the road and someone is following too closely behind you, obviously in a hurry, most people find that their first inclination is irritation with those trying to impose their will, which is for you to move out of their way. What you do not know is what is causing their hurry. They may be sick, racing to an emergency, late for an appointment, or maybe they are just a discourteous driver; regardless, you see their action, but do not know what precipitated their action. It is what you do not know, the space before their action, the space that you did not see, that is more than likely the cause of the tailgating in this scenario."

"Michael Jordan is wholeheartedly my favorite basketball player," the guru smiled. "I became a fan when he played in college and shot the game winning goal for the NCAA men's basketball championship as a freshman. My admiration carried forward as he began shooting the game winning goals for the Chicago Bulls, winning six NBA championships. Michael Jordan is the epitome of so many athletes. We, as spectators, see the product of what we have not seen. *What do you mean,* you may ask? Well, it has been said that Michael Jordan became better at playing basketball than everyone else by first becoming better at practicing basketball than everyone else. All of those minutes, hours, days, months, years of practice you did not see were exhibited on the court in what you did see. Once again, it is what you do not see that provides the importance to what you do see. What I like to call 'the space in between,' what you do not see, is much more significant than what you do see.

"Why have I brought this message to you today? Here is why, my good friends. Through every action there is a reaction of some sort, which leads to an action and reaction, which leads to another action, and on, and on, and on. So, a reaction *is* an action. Can we agree on that? Each of us go through every day based on a continuous action/ reaction basis - that is life. Remember, the actions and reactions of life are like a knife, they either serve you or cut you depending on if you grasp it by the handle or by the blade."

"You say, *Guru, you are talking in riddles.* I say no, for if you have ears, then hear. Because we live our lives based on action and reaction, the space in between the actions we take becomes the most important part of our lives." He paused purposefully. "Between every action there is a space of no action, which is the time of personal choice. This is what is meant by living in the moment. It is within this space, the space in between the action and reaction, the space when you have the freedom to make choices, that you create the scenarios that actually set up the next action/reaction - the proverbial domino effect. This means," he gazed meaningfully at his audience, "the choices you make during the space in between impact your future actions and reactions. The choices you make during the space in between can change the course of the future."

"I encourage each of you to live in the moment and make the space in between the focal point of your daily life. The world will be a far brighter place if each of us chooses to take control of the space in between and make positive choices that will in turn create our future actions and reactions to promote a brighter world. Think about it, within the space in between, each of us has an opportunity to control the initial path of a never ending set of falling dominoes called 'the action and reaction of life.'"

He continued, "It is within our control to speak a kind word instead of a harsh one, to offer a hand up instead of a push down, to hold out an open hand instead of a closed fist, to gaze with caring eyes instead of looking away. Life is all about choices, yours and mine, during the space between the actions, the space after the stimulus and before the response. There is an infinite number of possibilities leading from a single decision between actions and reactions."

"How many days are in a moment?" the guru inquired as he began the closure of his lecture. "How many weeks are in a day? How many years are in a month? Moments create days, which create weeks, which create months, which create years, but it all starts with a single moment. Who knows why people do certain things? These unexplainable actions are considered knee-jerk and made unconsciously. Our goal is to be and remain conscious. To be the person who is aware of the actions/ reactions around us and of the choices we are making during our time within the space in between. It is my hope that you will meditate on these final words and then act upon them, and meditate on them and then act on them, and so on. Remember in your comings and goings...

* * * * * * *

It's not what happens to you,

it's how you react to it.

* * * * * * *

* * * * * * *

Frick and Frack

* * * * * * *

Week Sixteen

The neighborhood biting flies, Frick and Frack, woke up early and began talking about the day ahead. The forest was alive with birds singing about the sunrise. Deer, squirrels, and rabbits were scurrying around, foraging for the last bits of sustenance before the sun came up...and before the humans came through for their regular morning walk. The humans were nice enough and never bothered anyone or anything, but the animals always kept their distance.

Frick and Frack observed all the ground activity before simultaneously deciding to buzz around to see who they could bite. Their first victim was a young deer. Once they had swooped down, deftly taken a nip out of her tender ear, and recovered from the dizzying flight through the air after having been shaken from their attacking place, they laid their aim on a fresh pile of dung. Frick and Frack were not sure who's doo they were doing, but it didn't matter. It was a great start to their day of malicious fun.

Hearing the distinctive voices of humans, they glanced knowingly at each other and rubbed their legs together in anticipation. Aggravating the humans always brought them so much joy!

Frick chuckled, "Here comes those folks from across the way. Let's go have some fun!"

"Come on!" Frack replied, wings vibrating to begin his ascent. They flew through the air with a trailing waft of stank coming from them.

As they buzzed forward, they heard the voice of the old horse fly, who was wise to their games, calling out to them, "Careful! Many hands those humans have."

"They can't hit what they can't see, you old *Yoda Breath!*" the boys called over their shoulders. When they were only yards away from the humans, they plunged in a nosedive to begin their assault with glee.

Buzzing the heads of the humans and creating misdirection was their favorite pastime. As usual, the humans, aggravatingly swatting this way and that, missed them with their errant swings. Frick and Frack quickly assessed their next assault and landed squarely on the back calf of each human; they just *loved* when the humans wore shorts. After nibbling their bare skin, they quickly let loose and flew upward, laughing as the humans jerked in response to the sting of their bites.

Frick and Frack continued to follow the humans around the edge of the woods in alternating dive-bombs. Just as expected, the humans continued to swing, but could never make any kind of contact as they bobbed and weaved around their bodies. Many times, the humans actually slapped themselves in their vain attempts to rid themselves of Frick and Frack. The flies laughed mercilessly as the humans self- inflicted more stings than the flies did with their bites.

Finally growing tired of their fun and games, Frick and Frack flew off for a siesta on a nearby oak leaf. "Oh, the joys of those early morning visits by the humans!" exclaimed Frack.

"Now for a little nap and then some more fresh doo nourishment before another woodland excursion," yawned Frick. "Who knows what might strike our fancy next."

Later that morning, some surprise visitors from the field strode into the edge of the woods to get out of the hot sun. Frick called over to Frack, who was just waking up from his morning nap, "Hey! Look over there. Fresh meat! Let's have some fun!"

Frack shook his head and, after taking in the sight of the two humans in the not too far off distance, said, "Bring it on!"

Taking off in reckless abandon, they made a beeline for the humans. In the blink of an eye, they began their assault. *First high, then low, then circle back for the coveted neck bite.* Hands were flying, limbs were jerking, and Frick and Frack actually weathered mini hurricane force winds that blew them slightly off course.

After steadying themselves, Frick grinned at Frack. "Man, that was great. Let's do it again!"

They zoomed in the opposite direction of the humans to pick up some speed, not to mention create the misconception that they would be pestering the humans no longer, then swerved right back to them. This time, Frick went high and Frack went low, totally confusing the humans who, this time, had all available hands swirling in an attempt to defend themselves from the aerial attack.

Sensing a high level of frustration from one of the humans in particular, Frick grazed his nose to land on his ear, laughing as the human's hand came down, missing Frick entirely, to smack himself. The burst of wind from his hand even gave Frick a great burst of air to "hang ten" on. Frack, seeing Frick's enjoyment, decided to copy his maneuver, except he buzzed one human in the face and then buzzed the other human on his ear. He could hear one human say to the other, "Stand still, I'll get him."

Frack landed on the one human for a millisecond before taking off in a burst of speed. The human swung, missing Frack, only to land with a smack on the other one. "Ouch! Did you get it?"

"No, missed him. Sorry!"

Frack circled around to where Frick was watching with glee and said, "Now that was great." The flies decided they'd had enough fun for a while and flew into the woods to see what else was going on.

That evening like clockwork, the humans from the morning came out for their walk around the field, which was next to the woods. Frick and Frack had been anxiously awaiting the humans as boredom had set in around midafternoon since they had had basically nothing to occupy their energy.

"All right, buddy," Frick said to Frack as they watched the humans from across the field, "let's create some mayhem."

"You got it. Remember, the first bite is the sweetest... I'll race you for it!" Frack called out as they buzzed forward in newfound speed.

Off they flew, silently approaching their unsuspecting prey with smiles on their faces. Eyes wide with excitement, they each headed toward a different human. Frick and Frack soon began their normal high-low-high attack strategy. As Frick ended his low attack and started back up for his high attack, which would end with a satisfyingly sweet bite, out of nowhere came a massive collision that left him dazed.

As he shook his head in an attempt to regain focus, he landed slowly on the neck of a human, and a resounding *smack* could be heard. Frick gasped as all of the air was knocked out of his body, and slowly fell from the human's neck to land solidly on the ground. He looked up to see the sole of a shoe lowering from the heavens to crush him into the earth.

Frack gasped in horror, immediately losing his own focus, as he saw Frick's broken body on the ground below. All of a sudden, he felt the full force and strength of the human hand and his lifeless body soon joined Frick's.

"Got 'em!" The humans continued their walk, discussing how they were so glad those aggravating biting flies were gone.

"I hate to kill things," one of them said.

"I do too," the other replied, "but those boys should have learned a long time ago that...

*   *   *   *   *   *   *

If you keep playing with <u>fire</u>
you are going to get <u>burned</u>.

*   *   *   *   *   *   *

*   *   *   *   *   *   *

Babble

*   *   *   *   *   *   *

Week Seventeen

"Michael, Gabriel, come forward." God motioned for his two faithful angelic beings to join him on his high throne. "Please share with me what you have seen in your most recent travels on Earth. You've both been gone for well over a season. What is it that mankind is up to these days? Have their actions improved since your last visit?"

While Michael and Gabriel made their way slowly up the celestial staircase, God noticed their heads were leaned close together as they conversed quietly with every step. Once they approached the majestic throne, they bowed low before the omnipotent one. "Rise, my faithful and trusted friends," God smiled. "Please sit at my feet and tell me what you have seen, heard, and learned from your Earthly comings and goings."

"Oh, great one," Michael shook his head in wonder, "the humans...they just never learn. They don't understand their evolution or even seem to know their history. They continue to make the same exact mistakes over and over again."

"Michael is right, my lord," Gabriel added. God's eyes shifted slowly to Gabriel's. "The humans have long forgotten that if they fail to know and understand their history, they are doomed to repeat it. And that is exactly what they are doing."

God stroked his chin thoughtfully. "Tell me, what are they doing...this time?"

"Well," Michael began, "you know, throughout history you have started over on more than one occasion in regards to the humans and the earth. If you remember, Gabriel and I helped the last time when Earth was flooded and only Noah, his family, and the animals were spared in the ark."

"Yes, that seems like it was just yesterday," God replied, his brow furrowed at the memory. "Of course, for me a thousand years seems to be a single day."

"Remember after the Great Flood when the people multiplied and filled the land? All of a sudden, they decided to build a massive tower to reach the heavens," Gabriel added.

"Yes," God chuckled sadly. "I never understood what they thought they would accomplish. For some reason they wanted to reach us to blame us for the discomfort, challenges, and problems they had brought into their own lives." He sighed. "That would not have been good for them. They had to learn to take ownership for their own actions and choices. I remember we decided to save the humans from themselves."

Gabriel said, "Almighty, if you recall, you originally planned to shake the foundations of the earth to cause the tower they were constructing to collapse, but Michael came up with the 'confusion' idea. You thought it was perfect as there would be no loss of physical life like with the Great Flood."

"We scrambled their ability to communicate so they couldn't understand each other," Michael replied.

God nodded, before saying quietly, "The humans even came up with a word for the tower to commemorate the moment they lost the ability to coherently communicate with each other. Babel. The Tower of Babel. Of course, the word they use for it now is 'babble.'"

"The reason we have brought this up," Michael started with a sigh, "is because they have come back full circle. This time, we believe it is worse than before."

God's eyebrows twitched in curiosity. "How so?"

Michael continued, "During the incident at the Tower of Babel, there were only about one thousand people that spoke the same language. Now there are billions of people with technology they have created and incorporated into every facet of their lives. The technology can translate languages from the sender to the receiver, making their ability to communicate as endless as their methods of communication."

"How many forms of direct communication do they now have?" God asked, his fingers lacing together.

"Let's see," Gabriel began, "there is verbal, written, and electronic, which can be activated with either mouth or hand."

"That's not too much." God's head tilted in contemplation. "Hand, mouth, and electronic...only three."

"Omnipotent one, that is just the start of it." Michael's eyes widened. "The problem is not only *how* they communicate, it is how they *deliver* the communication. It is immediate, instant, and can be sent all over the world in the blink of an eye. The humans have become giant antennas, receivers of any communication sent, whether true or false. They have developed all of these devices to communicate and there is absolutely no filter, no governor, except for themselves...if they actually *choose* to filter themselves."

Gabriel interjected, "Basically, if they think it, they communicate it. Some of the humans don't even give what they say a second thought. They just create their message and send it, sharing their opinions with everyone, whether they are knowledgeable about the content or not. They can type or say their message into a small device, press a button, and their message is then transported all over the world. It's unsettling that they have created an indirect means of communicating directly... and this type of communication has become the norm. They do this wherever they happen to be."

Michael turned back to God. "We must save them from themselves again."

"Do either of you have a plan to do this?"

"Well," Gabriel replied, "Michael and I have discussed this at great lengths. Thousands of years ago, we confused the language. What if we scramble the electronic signals they use to communicate? Their devices, which emit and receive electronic signals, will only show as vibrations and not be able to be deciphered into any type of communicable language."

"That is a solid plan," God said, nodding slowly. "But I have a better idea." The two angels stared at God expectantly. "We will do nothing."

Michael and Gabriel's faces were full of shock. Michael managed to choke out incredulously, "Nothing, my lord?"

God leaned forward on his throne. "Did you not say that they cannot discern between the correct and incorrect? What is true and what is false? From what you both shared, it appears they are already confused. We do not need to do anything to further confuse them because they have already done it to themselves. They do not know which way is up, partially because they choose not to look up."

"You see," God continued, "I have told them repeatedly 'that which has been is what will be, that which is done is what will be done, and there is nothing new under the sun.' I have told them to be quick to listen and slow to speak. From what you have shared, it seems like they do not listen...or maybe it's that they do not want to listen. Maybe they talk too much to listen. They talk with more than their mouths and speak with more than audible words."

"I have told them I created them with two ears and one mouth to listen twice as much as they speak," God shook his head in disappointment. "Now they speak with mouths, fingers, and eyes. They speak with a point and click. They speak with the touch of a key. It would appear to me that they have created their own confusion through their various forms of communication, which is their present day Tower of Babel. Now they hear as much with their eyes as they do with their ears. The Internet is just a giant classroom the world uses for passing around notes."

"But, Almighty," Gabriel pleaded, "if we do nothing, they will continue to make poor if not catastrophic decisions because of misinformation."

Michael added desperately, "And Earth may spin into chaos."

"You can lead a horse to water, but you cannot make it drink. The beings made in our likeness need to discover that *information is not knowledge and knowledge is not wisdom.* They need to understand that wisdom begins with reverence to the creator and the creation. The creator speaks in a still small voice. I am not sure how they will hear me, for as powerful as I am, I speak in a whisper. I'm not sure that they can hear my voice in their minds with all of their senses absorbed in this frenzied communication. It would appear to me that when they are ready for true knowledge and wisdom, they will have to...

*   *   *   *   *   *   *

Disconnect to truly connect.

*   *   *   *   *   *   *

*   *   *   *   *   *   *

Do and Say

*   *   *   *   *   *   *

Week Eighteen

What a campaign speech! It was absolutely unbelievable in its verbal charge! The crowd had been worked up into a frenzy! I was amazed. I had no idea this was what participating in a political rally was like, which was honestly very similar to sitting in the stands of a Florida college football game. The candidate preached energetically for over an hour informing his legion of followers of what his opponent had failed to do and of the actions he would take.

"We are going to lower taxes across the board," he stated with conviction and emotion. "We are going to strengthen our military presence and reinforce our borders. We are going to revamp the entire health care system. Change for the better is my promise to all of you!"

The roar of applause from the crowd was thunderous. I could only stare at him in awe. What a great orator; he was mesmerizing with his cadence. He held up his hands to hush the crowd before continuing. "I know many of you have struggles, particularly financial struggles: struggles to pay bills, struggles to maintain households, struggles to buy new clothes, struggles to buy healthy food, struggles with maintenance repairs, and struggles juggling all of your obligations."

I soon noticed his chin quivered slightly as he paused to wipe at a stray tear that rolled down his cheek. He drew in a deep, slow breath. "I feel your pain, I know you think you will never be able to retire, I know your shoulders are heavy and some of you feel as if you are carrying the weight of the world on them. Your strength is a quality of great admiration."

On and on, the candidate explained to all in the auditorium and those watching the televised event from their living rooms across the nation, how much heart he had for the people, how he believed in giving everyone a hand up, and how it was wrong for the "haves" to neglect the "have nots." I, just like all the others within ear shot, left the rally feeling we finally had a candidate that would help everyone, that would finally look out for the underdog, that would not take advantage of us, and would govern first and foremost by what would be in the best interest of the masses, the average everyday citizens, the folks that simply needed a "hand up."

The next morning at work, I received an emergency call regarding plumbing issues at the home address of 1 Unbelievable Way. The hard earned dollars I'd recently spent to create my website and referral base were really starting to pay off. As I keyed the address into my GPS, I wasn't exactly sure where I was going, but I knew for a fact it was in the wealthiest residential section of the city.

When I reached the thick iron gate that surrounded the property, I happened to glance at the mail box to my left, and, much to my amazement, realized I was in fact about to walk into my chosen candidate's residence! My heart thumped solidly in my chest as I buzzed the security pad to gain access. I was soon greeted by a security guard who gave me the once over and scanned the log book for what I assumed was scheduled appointments or guests. He checked me off before opening the gate.

As I slowly drove up the winding drive, I was blown away by the immaculate landscaping, fountains, and stone work. This residence did not contain a house, it housed a mansion, one that was quite impressive and frankly overpowering. I parked in front of the house in the circle drive, opened the back of my cargo van to grab my tool bag, and headed to the front door. Just as I reached out to press the doorbell, the oak door swung open to reveal what I assumed to be the housekeeper. She ushered me in and immediately directed me to the master bathroom. My eyes darted around quickly to take in all the fancy items, large paintings, and expensive furniture. I was once again in awe of this candidate, but now for a very different reason.

Stepping into the large bathroom, I quickly deduced the problem: a broken commode seal. I grabbed a wrench to loosen the bolts to lift the commode and repair the seal. My jaw hung open. I could not believe my eyes.

The toilet seat was gold!

Not wood painted gold or a gold laminate, but *gold.* Actual *14K gold.*

As I mechanically completed the repair, my thoughts raced back to the message of the campaign speech I'd been mesmerized with just the night before. Did I hear him wrong last night? I could've sworn he said he knew our struggles, and that he understood our financial issues. I scoffed. *Really? How can he understand anything I go through when he parks his tail on a golden toilet seat?*

I immediately pictured the candidate perched on his golden toilet seat, although it was more of a throne, laughing at the enthusiasm and praise the crowd gave him at the rally. Throne, yeah, that was an interesting synonym for toilet, and our candidate surely had a throne in his bathroom, while some of his supporters must surely spend time picking splinters from their butt once they get up off their old, worn out, wooden toilet seats.

I quickly cleaned up and left...disenchanted and disgusted. Driving away from 1 Unbelievable Way, I was reminded of the saying, "A picture is worth one thousand words." Snorting softly, I thought, *This was just the opposite — a picture* eliminated *one thousand words.*

On Sunday, I decided to stay home from church and catch a worship service on TV. I flipped through the stations until I came upon the televised service of Fire and Brimstone Evangelical Christian Fellowship out of Georgia. The worship service was quite stirring with congregational singing of classic gospel hymns and a beautiful choir special of "He Touched Me." The Reverend Robert Righteous delivered a passionate sermon centered on purity. Purity of mind, body, and spirit.

Pastor Righteous used Ephesians Chapter 5 from the Holy Bible for the basis of his sermon. As the spotlight shone off of his shiny bald head, the pastor preached, exclaimed, and exhorted from the pulpit. His wife sat to his right, affirming his words with nods and raised hands. The sermon ringing through the sanctuary caused the self-examination of every nook and cranny of the listeners' mind and spirit.

Pastor Righteous and his wife had moved the whole congregation, at least one thousand people, to kneel and pray to God for cleansing of any iniquity within them and their relationships. The message was so powerful even I found myself kneeling on my living room floor with arms outstretched and hands held high asking for God to examine me and cleanse me. The worship service ended with a tremendous benediction, with his final words being, "Now go amongst them and be pure."

That evening I received an emergency service call for plumbing issues from the "You Drop In" motel from the lower east side of the city. Once again, I wasn't sure of the exact location, but I did know the area was pretty sketchy. It was nowhere you wanted to be after the sun went down.

As I pulled into the motel parking lot, maneuvering to avoid pot holes along the way, I diligently surveyed the area and decided to lock my vehicle while I was in the motel office getting all the information and the room key. The night attendant explained that the problem was a clogged shower drain in Room 104 as he handed me the room key.

While I made my way to the room, I noticed there was a fairly new white Lexus with a Georgia license plate parked in front of Room 105. Once I opened the door to 104 and stepped through the threshold, it became very evident just how thin the walls that separated the two rooms. Although I vaguely recognized one of the voices, I shook my head in amusement. The couple in 105 seemed to be enjoying themselves immensely. *I sure am glad I'm not spending the night in here,* I thought while walking into the bathroom. *None us of would be getting any sleep!*

After checking on the tub drain, I realized the fix would be an easy one, which meant I would practically be in and out! I went back to the truck to get an industrial snake for the drain and smiled to myself. *I think I will have spent more time driving to the service call then the call would take; now that's good profit margin.*

As I turned back to walk into 104, the door to 105 creaked open to reveal a middle age man with dark sunglasses and a very obvious toupee. He rushed to the Lexus, unlocked the door, reached under the seat to pull out a brown bag, and headed back to his room.

I soon finished snaking the drain, then ran some hot water with a splash of drain opener for good measure. While I was locking the door to 104, I couldn't help but notice that the blinds to 105 were slightly open, allowing a clear view into the room. My bag crashed to the ground as I stood frozen in shock.

That man in the motel room was Pastor Righteous, and the woman he was with was definitely *not* his wife! I knew I recognized his voice! The thud of my tool bag hitting the concrete prompted both of their heads to whip toward the sound. There were beads of sweat dripping off his shiny bald head now that the toupee was off, and there was no denying that they were having a "religious experience" of their own. It appeared to be much more involved than a prayer meeting.

"Oh God!" I heard him exclaim as I hastily bent down to retrieve my bag. "Shut the blinds!"

I quickly returned the key and headed to my work van, glancing once more at 105 to see the blinds completely closed. Shaking my head in disgust, I thought to myself, *Pastor Righteous may be able to "talk the talk," but he doesn't have a clue about how to "walk the talk."*

Pondering over the events and revelations of the last two days, a billboard soon caught my eye as I drove home. I pulled over onto the shoulder of the road to take a picture of the message as it fully summed up the revelation I had discovered. It read...

*   *   *   *   *   *   *

What you <u>do</u> is so loud

I cannot hear what you <u>say</u>.

*   *   *   *   *   *   *

*   *   *   *   *   *   *

How You See It

*   *   *   *   *   *   *

Week Nineteen

My eyes quickly scanned over the email my wife sent minutes earlier. She asked if I wanted to go ahead and make a payment on our only credit card because it was inching toward the limit. Not very long ago she had wisely requested to receive electronic notification when we were within three hundred dollars of reaching the limit. This was a result of unknowingly hitting our limit and then attempting to pay for a meal at one of our usual spots, and...well, it made us a little red in the face when we had to change our form of payment.

We began using our credit card for all monthly expenses due to a wonderful cash back rewards program. Accordingly, we made sure to pay off the balance every month or we would defeat the purpose of using the credit card as the interest charges would offset the rebates. Several times a year, we would crowd the card limit prior to the payment due date. This happened to be one of those times. My fingers typed out a quick reply asking her to transfer several hundred dollars as an out of cycle payment before we paid off the balance in full at the end of the month, as usual.

After working for several more minutes during the afternoon drag, I stepped out of my office in search of liquid fuel. I poured myself a cup of coffee, noting the office was almost out of coffee cups. A quick glance at my watch reinforced the fact that I had plenty of time to make a dash to the grocery store in preparation for tomorrow. That would work in my favor since I'd been planning to stop at the roadside flower stand right around the corner from the grocery store to purchase some autumn mums for my yard after work.

I wrapped up a few loose ends at the office before driving the few blocks to the grocery store. Pulling into a somewhat close parking space, I walked briskly from my car into the store, strode halfway down aisle nine, grabbed the coffee cups, and made my way to the checkout lanes. The gum on the convenience racks along the checkout aisle called my name. Unable to resist, I tossed a few packs on the belt alongside the coffee cups while I waited for the woman ahead of me to finish paying for her groceries.

The cashier soon rang up my purchase and stated the total. I pulled out my credit card and inserted it into the chip reader payment terminal. After typing in my concurrence on the amount and then my PIN, the transaction went through and I swiftly grabbed my bag of items before heading to my vehicle and driving to the roadside flower stand that was just around the corner. I couldn't wait to see the selection of mums, knowing they would add to the fall decor of my yard.

I slowly eased my vehicle into the little gravel parking lot before quickly exiting to peruse the mums. Almost immediately, my eyes spied the two mums I wanted to purchase. Their vibrant yellow flowers were symmetrical and would be beautiful positioned at any angle near my pumpkins and gourds. I grabbed the mums and placed them on the checkout stand for payment.

"Did you find everything you were looking for?" the cashier asked while ringing up the flowers.

"I did," I responded, pulling out my credit card once more, "thank you."

"Two mums will be ten dollars," she stated, and I handed her my card.

"Thank you, sir. Oh, let me see..." She checked the drawer under the register before glancing at me apologetically. "I don't think the manager left the tablet for taking card payments."

"Let me check my wallet," I said thumbing through quickly in hopes of finding the amount in cash. I sighed, taking the card from her outstretched hand. "Sorry, I just don't carry cash anymore. Let me go to an ATM and I'll come back before you close."

"Wait a second," she said nicely, "let me call the manager and see if she can process your card information by phone."

"Thank you very much. I really appreciate that."

She called the manager, explained the situation, and then asked, "Do you want to take the information?" She handed me the phone saying, "She can process the payment, but wants the information directly from you."

I held the phone up to my ear. "Hello?"

On the other end of the phone, a very pleasant voice sounded. "I am so sorry for the inconvenience, but I can help you complete your purchase."

"Thank you," I sincerely replied.

"If you're ready, I can take your card information now," she said, and I went on to share the card information, expiration date, and my zip code. Then she asked, "And what is the security code, sir?" I flipped the card over and read, "6 – 1 – 0."

There was a long sigh from the other end of the line. "I'm so sorry, I must have typed something in wrong. It did not take the transaction. Can you please give me the information again? I am so sorry."

"It's not a problem," I said, and restated the card number, expiration date, and zip code once more. "And the security code is 6 – 1 – 0."

"Huh, something's wrong; it did not take. I must not be keying something in correctly." She paused for a moment.

I know there's room under the card's limit, I thought to myself in confused concern. And I just used it not more than ten minutes ago for a purchase of less than ten dollars! What's going on?

"Tell you what," the manager sighed, "let's try this one more time. You read it to me, and as I type it in I am going to repeat it back to you."

"Sounds good," I nodded to myself. "Ready?"

"Yes."

We went through the same process as before, except this time she repeated every single digit back to me. Flipping the card over to state the security code, I began to read the same numbers, "6 – 1 – 0," when the young cashier suddenly held out her hand.

"Excuse me, sir" she began politely, "may I see your card for just a second? I think I know the problem."

"Absolutely," I handed her the card.

She studied it for a moment before turning it to face me and pointing to the numbers. "Here is the security code: 0 – 1 – 9."

I chuckled, reading the actual number in disbelief. "Thank you," I said to her before directing my words back to the manager. "The security code is 0 – 1 – 9, not 6 – 1 – 0. Sorry, I guess I can't see today!"

The manager laughed. "Well, that did it! The transaction took and you will have an email receipt forwarded to the email of record on the card. Thank you so much for your business. Have a wonderful day."

"Thanks, you too." Returning the phone back to the clerk, I smiled. "And thank you for helping me."

She nodded with a grin. "You're welcome, sir."

Just as I was about to slide the card back into my wallet, I glanced down at the security code once more, shaking my head in disbelief. The digits were clearly "0 – 1 – 9." *Where in the world did I get "6 – 1 – 0" from?*

The cashier happened to catch my eye and said ever so politely, "Sir, you flipped your card over so you were reading the numbers upside down."

Smiling as I finally tucked the card away, I said, "Well, that just goes to show you...

*   *   *   *   *   *   *

How you <u>see</u> it really depends on how you <u>look</u> at it

*   *   *   *   *   *   *

* * * * * * *

Appearances

* * * * * * *

Week Twenty

Come in my friends and, please, have a seat," said Guru Garysheema.

Never one to miss one of his profound seminars, I beamed as soon as I saw that super cool swami and nodded to him with deep respect as I took my seat. After glancing around the room, I sighed somewhat in relieved satisfaction. *It's another full house, as usual,* I thought. *I'm glad I got my ticket early.* I had also noticed that this room was a more intimate setting than normal, which I assumed was the reason that each of his ten scheduled sessions held over the course of the weekend were capped at twenty people.

The guru sat on a stool behind a table holding various water pitchers. Each had its own unique style and was decorated differently. There was gold, silver, ceramic, clear glass...but the final water pitcher, the one made of stone, was the odd duck in the varied line up. While the others were sleek, shiny, and beautifully designed, that one was unappealing and visibly chipped.

The ugly stone one really stands out and it's not for aesthetics like the other ones. Knowing how the guru likes to teach, I'm sure there's a lesson surrounding the old ugly chipped stone one, but who knows; he keeps you guessing. They actually could be used to hold some form of liquid. It does seem a tad bit warm in our room, and I really hope this isn't one of those sweat lodge deals. Even if this "steam" room turns into a "stink" room, hearing Guru Garysheema just speak will be worth it.

"First, I would like to extend the warmest welcome to you all, and I do mean 'warm,'" the guru chuckled while fanning himself. He smiled at each member of the seminar before extending his arms outward in a sweeping motion directed toward the water pitchers. "Please, everyone, come forward and touch the water pitcher that you feel yourself drawn to. There is no right or wrong answer, as this deals with personal taste. This is not first come, first serve since there are plenty of pitchers of each design under the table. Do not over think. Simply select the one that you would like to carry home with you at the conclusion of today's gathering."

All twenty of us approached the table in an orderly fashion. When we each stood before the guru, we touched the water pitcher we liked. He reached under the draped table to retrieve a water pitcher identical to the one that was selected. The gold pitcher was a big hit followed by the ceramic one, which was my preferred water pitcher, then the clear glass one, and finally the silver one. The lonely water pitcher, as one would expect, was the chipped stone one.

Once the last person returned to their seat, Guru Garysheema smiled at us all again. "My friends, it makes me happy to see so many familiar faces as well as a few new faces. Life appears to be treating you all well. And just as life *appears* to be treating you well, today we will talk about *appearances.*"

"All of you know that appearances are often deceiving. It has been said many times that 'you cannot judge a book by its cover.' You have heard 'beware of a wolf in sheep's clothing.' How about 'dress for success,' or 'all that glitters is not gold?' Life is all about appearances and how we must be wary of them." He chuckled slightly and shook his head in bewilderment. "No matter how many times we are told this, time and time again our first natural response is to seek what is appealing to our senses. We are drawn to appearances."

"Do we put more emphasis on what is pleasing on the exterior than on the substance of the interior?" He paused, gazing around the room, allowing the question to sink in. "How many of you know the story from the Holy Bible when God instructed Samuel to choose the next king of Israel?" I noticed several hands raised along with my own.

"For those of you who aren't familiar, the story goes like this: Samuel, God's prophet to the people, lined up the men of Israel and attempted to choose the next king by the outward appearance of the men as they marched by him. God said to Samuel, 'Do not look at the appearance or height. The Lord does not see as man does. For man sees the outward appearance, but the Lord sees the heart.' As one of my favorite cartoon animals Scooby Doo would say, 'Ruh-ro.'" The guru paused with a smile to allow the many listeners to finish their snickers at the fact that this profound man actually watched 'Scooby Doo.' He continued, "That should get your attention."

"In this world," he held up his hands, "we are drawn to the bright, to the shiny, to the flamboyant, to the new, to the bells, to the whistles. We are drawn to what screams at us for attention. Look at our media. Look at what is glamorized. We tend to gravitate to what attracts our senses. Companies manipulate this all the time with flashing lights in casinos, red and orange in restaurants, laugh tracks on TV shows, and mood music in offices. A thunderstorm is now 'severe weather,' and the most recent news report is now 'breaking news.'"

"Youth, beauty, and physique are idolized, and marketing techniques use these qualities to sell their products with the subliminal message, 'If you buy this product, you will be desirable too.' Magazines are dedicated to revolve around celebrities, fashion icons, and the latest trends – what we as a society have deemed glamourous and the epitome of ultimate success. Of course, what is described in these articles is the glitter, the glamor, and positive spin to promote these figures, companies, and trends to make them more appealing."

The temperature in the room seemed to rise with every passing second, and I soon found myself beading with sweat. Investigating the room, I saw everyone else was beginning to show the same effects. The guru stood and said, as if reading our collective thought, "It is getting a little warm in here, don't you think? Would anyone care for some water?" Almost every single hand shot up in the air simultaneously. He chuckled, reaching for the ugly stone water pitcher. "Well, I am certainly glad each of you have your own water pitcher."

His gaze shifted away from us. "Can we please roll in the water and bring in the cups?"

From the side of the conference area, several large water vats with taps were wheeled in while cups were passed out to us with the instruction to set them under our chairs. We sat on the edge of our seats, sweat running down our faces, attempting to wait patiently to fill our pitchers. The guru was not in a hurry to relieve us from the heat, but something told me there was another reason he'd reveal later.

As his eyes wandered over our flushed faces, I was positive he could actually hear the splatter of sweat dripping from our nose and chins to form small puddles on the floor. *Of course,* I thought inwardly, using the sleeve of my shirt to wipe at my face, *when you get something on your mind that has to do with comfort, the seconds turn into long minutes and the minutes turn into long hours. It's funny how the speed of time is fluid in that way. Mmm, fluid. I'm definitely ready for water.*

Finally, Guru Garysheema nodded to us. "Please form three lines in front of the three kegs and proceed to fill your pitchers." There was a collective sigh of relief as we quickly stood, methodically moving to the water dispensers to fill our pitchers. As the first three pitchers were filled, the guru instructed for each of us to count to ten at the front of the room before returning to our seats.

As each of us began our count to ten, it became quite obvious that some of the pitchers had cracks and would not hold much water; in fact, it appeared that *all* of the pitchers had cracks and were dripping, some fast, some slow, but all were dripping. *Everyone had better hurry up and get back to their seat to fill up the cup so they can drink some water!* I thought, halfway to ten and halfway to losing all of my water to the floor.

Some people didn't even wait to get back to their seat; they turned the pitcher up on its end and drank, but, of course, more went on their shirt or top than their mouth. I noticed many people grimaced after they finished their drink. By the time most returned to their seats, there were only a few drops left in the bottom of their pitchers and no matter how they tried to stop the pitcher from leaking...it didn't.

By the time I made it back to my seat, I still had a decent amount left in my pitcher, but certainly nowhere near as much as when I started. Reaching under my seat for the cup, I filled it and brought it eagerly to my mouth for a coveted drink. As soon as the water hit my tongue, a chalky taste filled my mouth. Yuck! Forcing myself to swallow, I dumped the remaining water from the cup back into the pitcher. Looking around, I could see many were staring in disbelief and irritation at the water in their water pitchers.

Everyone was staring intently at the guru. My eyes widened when I realized his ugly, cracked stone pitcher was not leaking, and he appeared to enjoy the water he so elegantly sipped on. Beaming, he toasted us with his cup. It was not reciprocated. Guru Garysheema stood and smiled. "What have you learned today, my friends?" Everyone was silent.

"You have learned," he continued, motioning to his stone pitcher, "that, once again, appearances can be deceiving. When I asked each of you to pick a water pitcher, you all picked the prettier ones, the shinier ones, the slicker ones. No one investigated the structure of the pitchers or checked to see if cracks were there, which could only be seen by looking inside the pitcher. Not a single one of you chose the old roughed up one. What you have discovered about your pretty water pitcher, your shiny water pitcher, your slick water pitcher is that form should always follow function. Yes, they are very beautiful...very nice to look at. But they did not hold water very well. They also leached the flavor of your water, some more than others depending on the water pitcher you chose."

Everyone nodded in understanding.

"Now, this stone water pitcher may not be the most beautiful water pitcher to look at, but it fulfills its purpose time and time again, year after year. While your pretty pitchers, shiny pitchers, and slick pitchers are beautiful to look at, they are not as reliable as the stone pitcher that still fulfills its purpose even after receiving many cracks over the years. It is reliable not because of its appearance, but because of its function. After all, it is not the water pitcher itself that matters, it is what the pitcher holds that matters."

"Everyone, please come forward and bring your cups. I will pour you all some water from my chipped stone water pitcher. As you drink your water, contemplate how water pitchers can teach us about all the appearances in life. Every time you look at your chosen water pitcher from here on out, my friends, may you always be reminded to...

* * * * * * *

Love the pitcher less

and the water more.

* * * * * * *

Best

Week Twenty-One

Floating upward...

Up, up, and up into the light...

The brilliant, all-encompassing light...

Light that is amazingly bright but not blinding... Inviting...

Heavenly.

Looking down, I can see myself on the ground as the emergency technicians feverishly work on my body. I'm not sure what had happened, but all of a sudden, I'd felt faint and then a strange floating sensation filled my body...the same one I'm feeling now...and then I was high above everything.

And this light...

I'm drawn upward, upward into this light...

A light with open arms...

A light of acceptance...

A light of warmth and love...

I can feel it through my entire being. But I don't just feel it... I *know* it.

Briefly glancing down once more, I wave goodbye to my body as I continue making my way into the light. Not at all understanding what's propelling me forward, I willingly follow the call of the light. Even if I had a choice, I would still follow this beautiful guiding beacon anywhere.

The voice I hear as I approach the light is not audible, but I can hear it within my being. The voice or vibration is soft but loud. Gentle but firm. A whisper and a shout. "Come, my child, come."

I am within the light. It is encompassing me, consuming me, and illuminating every particle of my essence.

"Are you ready to come home? Was life all that you dreamed it would be?" The questions resonate within my being. Contemplating before answering, I can see the events of my life flash before me. How utterly amazing that thirty years' worth of emotions, events, and memories can be absorbed in the blink of an eye.

I respond with my thoughts, "I think so and not exactly."

"My child, you think you are ready to come home, but you are not sure about your life? Is that how you feel?" Though this was formed as a question, I felt the light's compassion.

"It was so fast and I really didn't amount to much."

"Speed is relative," comes the very calm reply. "What is your measurement of value?"

"I wasn't successful and I pretty much failed at everything I tried. I just never seemed to measure up to others and couldn't manage to be who I wanted to be."

"Why didn't you become *you?*" says the steady voice. "Why didn't you become all that *you* are?"

"Why didn't you help me when I prayed to you?" I respectfully question.

The voice's gentle response cuts through to my very core. "I am here to help you be all *you* can be, not to help you be someone else."

"Others were smarter, stronger, and faster than me. You blessed them more than you blessed me."

As the voice speaks, my entire being is wrapped lovingly in acceptance. "Do not compare yourself or your dreams to others. Success is doing the best *you* can with what you have wherever *you* are."

"But – " Before I can complete the thought, I'm engulfed with accountability.

"Reaching your God-given potential requires taking responsibility for yourself and your life. It is up to you to use hard work and determination to accentuate your God-given strengths and talents."

I am consumed in thought.

Suddenly, the light opens below me and I'm encouraged to gaze down at a beautiful flower garden. "I am sending you back, my child. It is not your time yet. Remember what I have shared with you. Now, look at the flowers below. See their individual beauty just as a butterfly does when it chooses where to land. Take in their collective beauty as a camera does when capturing a moment. Embrace their unique colors and patterns like an artist when composing a masterpiece. Notice their textures like a bee as they pollenate others. As you go back to life, *remember.*

I float down, down, down...

Ever so gently...

Leaving the light that is so loving.

The still small voice fills my being once more to give me a final instruction for life. "Remember, my child the lesson of the flower...

* * * * * * *

A flower doesn't think of competing

with those next to it,

it simply blooms.

* * * * * * *

* * * * * * *

The Worry Gang

* * * * * * *

Week Twenty-Two

The Worry Gang traveled silently through the office complex, plotting and scheming as to who they could attack next. Passing by dozens of opened office doors, they listened in on the conversations between employees and peered over people's shoulders to read their emails. After gathering intelligence about every employee throughout the company, they found just the right person to mess with: Brad Workman, the division manager of the company.

They overheard him explain to his wife over the phone that if the company did not hit their profitability numbers this quarter, the CEO and Board of Directors would more than likely ask for his resignation. They heard his wife say, "Oh, honey, don't worry. You built that division from the ground up; it makes more money for that company than all of the other divisions combined! You're just going to stress yourself out."

Brad sighed heavily. "You just don't understand. It has become a 'what have you done for us lately' type of mentality around here, and if I can't – "

His wife gently interrupted Brad's worries. "Breathe, just breathe and calm down. Get up and out of your office. Walk around a little and I think you will feel better."

"You're right. Maybe I'll just go to the gym early and work all of this out of my system." Brad ran a hand over his face. "Thanks, honey. I will see you this evening."

As Brad turned to his computer to key into the electronic employee calendar that he would be out of the office for the next hour, the Worry Gang seized the opportunity to pounce. They settled heavily on his shoulders to whisper in his ear.

"Are you sure you want to do this?" they hissed. "You might better stay and grind out some more work so the powers that be don't think you're just cruising along. You know they are watching you. They have spies in your office... Haven't you noticed every time you log out of your computer and turn the light out in your office, people in the other offices watch when you walk by? They are keeping tabs on you. Are you sure you want to do this? It'll be one more thing for them to whisper about as you walk out the door..."

Brad shook his head. *Stop,* he ordered himself, *stop with all of this.* Pushing up from his desk, Brad switched off his office light and began heading down the hall. All of a sudden, a voice called out from one of the side offices.

"Brad, will you be back today?" asked Ken, one of the junior project managers.

"Certainly," Brad replied in annoyance. "I'm *just* taking an early lunch. Is that *okay* with you?"

"Well, excuse me!" Ken stepped out of his office to confront Brad's obvious snark. "I was just trying to make sure we had the proper coverage this morning if you were going to be out."

"I'm sorry," Brad offered sincerely. "Don't pay any attention to me. I've not been sleeping well and it's showing. Sorry."

"No worries," Ken waved as he turned back to his office. "It happens to the best of us."

Brad soon stepped out of the building with the Worry Gang perched deftly on his shoulders. "We told you," they mocked. "They are *watching* you. They are out to get *you.* They are waiting for you to *slip up.* And don't let Ken's nice guy persona fool you. He only wants your position. He's tired of waiting for his turn to have the big job in the company. He is gunning for you, just waiting for you to make a fatal move. He knows it's coming. He knows it's only a matter of time."

Blowing out a large exhale, Brad quickened his pace as he made his way down the couple of blocks to his gym. He knew a hard workout was just what he needed to take his mind off all the stuff bouncing around in his mind...if only for an hour. The slight relief Brad felt as his feet stepped through the threshold of the gym doors almost knocked the Worry Gang off his shoulders. As soon as he scanned his membership card at the front, Brad's eyes landed on the TVs in the aerobics area, several of which were showing CNBC.

All of a sudden, a ribbon stating *BREAKING NEWS* streamed across the screens. Brad's heart skipped a beat as he saw ABCD, the stock symbol for his company, showing a big red arrow pointing down with a huge *20%* beside it. Brad froze. *Oh no, the stock is down twenty percent! This is not good, not good at all.*

The Worry Gang clawed its way up until they were wrapped around Brad's neck. "The company is going to cut!" they hissed in both of his ears. "The company is going to cut! *You're fifty years old.* They are going to cut *you!* They can pay that thirty-year-old *half* of what they pay you *and* his benefits package will be less. That means cost savings to the company and increases to net income."

Perspiration rolled down the inside of Brad's upper arms as he continued to stare blindly at the screens. *I need to get back to the office. I can't workout now! What if the Regional Vice President calls and I'm not in?* Beads of sweat dotted his forehead. *Calm down. Remember what Jane said. Just breathe.* Brad's chest tightened in another bout of anxiety. *Lord held me, Cindy's college tuition payment is coming up soon, there's that mortgage payment that never goes away, not to mention still paying for Christmas...* He swallowed hard. *Well, there will be severance and vacation pay – that should get me through a couple of months. The job market is okay right now, but I don't want to have to move.* Brad's head continued to spin round and round while the Worry Gang chuckled in amusement.

Brad blinked rapidly, startled to find himself staring into an empty locker. His mind was so clouded with gloom and doom he didn't even remember walking through the gym into the locker room. Brad decided since he was already at the gym and in the locker room to go ahead and change. He'd get on the elliptical machine for thirty minutes or so to try and work some anxiety out of his system. The Worry Gang changed into their workout clothes and hung tight with Brad as he headed to the Matrix elliptical.

About twenty minutes into Brad's workout, he glanced up and noticed that all seven of the aerobic room's TVs were playing the local news channel. Reading the subtitles, Brad became interested in the local economic forecast. *Unemployment on the rise,* read the subtitle.

Brad felt a tight knot form in the pit of his stomach. *Forty-five to sixty year olds feeling the brunt of the unemployment and underemployment trends,* it continued to read. The knot shot from his stomach to his throat. He tried in vain to swallow against it.

The Worry Gang beamed. They were having a field day with Brad! They had definitely chosen the right victim. The more Brad attempted to put out the fire of worry, the more they fanned the flames. Finally, with two minutes left on the elliptical workout, Brad couldn't take it anymore. He decided to stop, get cleaned up, and head back to the office. There was no use in avoiding the inevitable when it seemed to be everywhere. The Worry Gang hung heavy on his sweat-soaked shirt as he trudged back to the locker room.

As Brad walked back to the office, his mind traveled to the early years of his career and soon he thought of all the accomplishments he had made. The more he focused on the positives of his thirty-plus year career, the looser the grip of the Worry Gang became.

"Hold on, guys," the leader of the Worry Gang ordered to the others. "He's trying to shake us off. Dig deep! Hold tight! Don't let loose of him!"

As always, Brad strode past the elevator to climb the steps to his fourth floor office. He started off taking one step at a time, but as soon as he reached the second floor indicator the Worry Gang felt a definite shift, causing them to slide a little further down Brad's shoulders. Brad squared his shoulders, puffed out his chest, and drew in a deep breath.

"Bring it on," he said aloud and began taking two steps at a time. Brad grinned to himself. He felt as if he were finally channeling some of that swagger he'd relied upon to climb the corporate ladder. *Stay determined.* The door to the fourth floor was in sight. *Stay focused.*

Soon stepping into his office, he retrieved the most recent profit and loss statement for his division. As he surveyed the expense items, he zeroed in on the column that reflected other expenses. Focusing on the itemization within the column, one category caught Brad's eye. *Hmm,* he thought, leaning in closer, *what is that?* Brad immediately picked up the phone and called the warehouse manager to ask him about the additional storage charges shown in the category.

After discovering the storages charges had been increased because of an automatic escalator clause overlooked by corporate finance in the lease agreement when the lease had originally been negotiated, Brad dove into work. The Worry Gang whispered from over his shoulder. "You cannot do anything about that — it is in the contract. What will you actually be able to do? Don't even try."

Shaking his head to clear his thoughts, Brad placed a call to the Real Estate Management Company and discussed the escalator clause. After several conference calls throughout the day between Brad and the Real Estate Management Company, he was able to negotiate a fifty percent reduction in the automatic escalator payment. During the entire negotiation process, the Worry Gang's whispers soon turned into shouts full of doubts and reasons why it couldn't or wouldn't work. But the entire time, Brad continued to shake off the Worry Gang. Slowly but surely, their grip loosened and they fell to the ground with a *thud!*

Brad phoned his Regional Vice President and advised that at the beginning of next quarter his division would report a twenty percent *increase* in profitability due to his renegotiation on storage expense. The Regional Vice President was elated and congratulated Brad on a job well done. The Worry Gang raised the white surrender flag of defeat and scurried from Brad's office in shame, all the while searching for another victim to pounce on. Brad's head whipped to the side, thinking he noticed some movement on the carpet in the doorway of his office.

After hanging up the phone from the conversation with his boss, Brad pushed away from his desk, leaned back in his chair, and smiled to himself. *Wow,* he thought with satisfaction, *what a day. Once again, worry met its match because...*

* * * * * * *

Positive <u>action</u> defeats worry every time.

* * * * * * *

What You Know

Week Twenty-Three

After helping clear the dinner table, I walked into the den and turned on the TV to catch up on national news and world events. I'd been traveling most of the week and really hadn't paid much attention to what was going on in the world. Of course, what was news today was normally a distant memory by tomorrow afternoon. Regardless, I did try to stay abreast of current events and happenings in order to make informed decisions based on the best possible information I could gather.

The anchor for the twenty-four hour news channel was discussing several events on the national and global front while consulting a panel of three experts. Each of these individuals were loaded with prestigious credentials including educational and practical experience both past and present. After observing a few minutes of the discussion, my eyebrows raised in slight amusement. The anchor was serving a dual purpose: facilitator and moderator.

The subject matters for the roundtable forum included the correlation of extreme weather conditions and global warming, international tension created by the proliferation of nuclear weaponry, social and economic inequalities created by ethnic orientation, and the standard Washington D.C. conservative-liberal gridlock.

As each topic was thoroughly discussed across the panel, it became quite obvious that each expert's opinion outweighed the number of facts and research they presented. At the beginning of each topic, the moderator circled the table and inquired to what each expert *thought* this or that meant, or why they *thought* someone said this or that, and why they *thought* this or that happened.

Now, the three individuals speaking from the roundtable certainly appeared to be very intelligent and well informed on each issue, but I honestly didn't care what they personally *thought* about any of these topics. Everyone has an opinion and with an opinion comes a bias, which meant, for all practical purposes, the discussion becomes conjecture.

Instead of hearing about the issues themselves, I was hearing about what several individuals *thought* about the issues.

As I continued to analyze the forum, I soon noticed the moderator began asking the experts what they had heard about the topic at hand. Listening closer, I came to realize he was basically asking if they had inside knowledge of various aspects of each topic.

Now, I wasn't throwing stones, but that seemed to be inching close to tabloid reporting often seen in the checkout lines at grocery stores. Gossip. *Come on,* I thought to myself in awe, *what you heard? We all know what you hear is a function of who you hear it from, and that is a function of the filters and perspectives of the one that is relaying the information. The first thing that comes to mind is the old grade school exercise where the teacher whispers a statement to the first student and then it's whispered into the ear of each student in the class until the final student stands up and tells the class what they heard, which invariably is different than what the teacher actually said.*

Instead of hearing about the issues, I was hearing what an individual had or had not *heard* about the issues.

Honing in even more on the forum was the fact that each of the experts began to quote various articles and publications to support their assertions and positions. I knew intelligent debates typically required a basis of authority, but I was struggling to find the validity of the quotes from this source or that source... particularly when I had no idea who or what the source may or may not be. There were some sources I was familiar with, but overall, I couldn't recall the existence of most periodicals nor authors or researchers.

Instead of hearing about the issues, I was hearing about what an expert had *read* about a certain subject. And, quite frankly, I could read for myself.

I leaned back in my chair as the roundtable forum began to wrap up. My brow furrowed. I was struggling with what I'd just heard. This was supposed to be *news* — facts, whole facts, and nothing but those facts. I wasn't sure this met my definition. It was bad enough that each news network put their own spin on what they reported, whether it be conservative, liberal, or somewhere in between. There were already enough hidden agendas within these programs that they certainly didn't need to toss into the mix what an accredited individual merely thought, heard, or read. Nevertheless, it certainly appeared in all of the broadcasted news channels, and, more times than not, the newscast consisted of what people thought, heard, or read.

The gears in my mind were spinning rapidly. *You know, everyone has an opinion...and they are not newsworthy. Opinions are like assumptions. When someone assumes and someone else acts on what someone else assumes, the result can easily make an ASS out of U and ME. Report the facts with no opinion and let the viewer process and decide without being coached one way or the other.* They were trying to make me believe something by what they thought, heard, or read. I don't want to *believe* something, I want to *know* something.

At the conclusion of the Round Table discussion, the network anchor requested comments to be directed to their network's email address and social media accounts; I jotted down the email address. After pondering more about the "news programming" I had just viewed, I decided to let the network know how I, as a viewer, felt. Once my fingers had finished typing, the mouse hovered over *Send* as I reread the phrase my father once shared with me. He said...

* * * * * * *

It's not what you think,

It's not what you heard,

It's not what you read,

It's what you know.

* * * * * * *

Looking Through The Windows

Week Twenty-Four

As I stepped into the kitchen, I noticed my father staring through the window as the farmer was plowing the fields beside and behind our new home. It had been an unusually dry winter and dust was flying everywhere. The windy March day didn't help either. My backyard appeared to have been plucked straight out of the Depression Era Dust Bowl.

"He's sure stirring everything up, isn't he?" I mused.

My father nodded. "He sure is. It's mighty dry out there. He's going to have to let it rain before he plants."

Once I'd poured myself a cup of coffee, I sat down opposite him at the kitchen table. My father had come to visit for a week or so to help us get situated in our new home. I was glad he was up before I went to work so we could talk. He was starting to look a little older to me these days. Of course, some of those added lines may have been more of a product of his half-empty view of the world than his age. You know, expression lines etch a little deeper as one ages.

Dad and I were quite different in how we viewed the world. I'd always enjoyed laughing, joking, and making light of things, but he always veered toward cynicism and slight paranoia as if everyone always had an ulterior motive. I tried to help him view situations and events from a slightly different angle.

Sometimes it worked. Sometimes it didn't.

"Dad, I hope you have a good day today," I paused to take a sip of coffee. "Anything special on your agenda?"

"Not particularly," he replied. "I think I will just see how many honey do's I can mark off of Ellen's list." My father was extremely handy, a talent that I had not acquired. Whenever he came to visit, my wife always had list of items that needed to be tightened or adjusted — the type of projects that he was so good at. Dad really enjoyed himself while completing them since they made him feel useful.

While I finished up my coffee, he glanced out the window and noted how the grass was not very green this year, even appearing a little gray. "There is nothing like that rich green bursting through the earth in the spring — that green always puts a smile on my face. But that gray out there...it kind of bums me out." He turned back to me. "You might better stop and get some Grow Green lawn fertilizer on your way home today, and we can spread it over your lawn tomorrow."

Of course I would. I certainly didn't want anything to deflate his spirits while he was staying with us, even though I personally didn't see the point in it. I nodded, getting up from my place at the table to rinse out my coffee mug. "Will do."

"You know, while you are at it, how about get a little TSP cleaner from the hardware store when you buy the Grow Green."

"TSP?" I queried, setting my mug into the dishwasher.

"Yes," he twisted around in his chair to meet my questioning gaze. "TSP mixed with a little bleach makes an excellent cleaner. It brightens things up."

"Right," I replied slowly, "but I'm not following."

"Son," Dad said in awe, "just look at your utility building back there." He pointed toward the window. "The beige vinyl siding looks brown. You want it bright and clean."

My brow furrowed slightly. I hadn't noticed the vinyl looking brown while I was out there yesterday, and I was pretty observant. But it would take more energy to argue my point against his. "Got it," I stated dryly.

As Ellen walked into the kitchen, I kind of rolled my eyes at her. She nodded in understanding. My father had a real knack for micromanaging.

"Good morning," she smiled cheerfully. "I hope everyone slept well and had pleasant dreams."

As Ellen began to pour herself a cup of morning coffee, my father turned to her. "Ellen, by chance have you changed the brand of clothes washing detergent you have been using?"

"Well, no," she responded. "Why do you ask?"

"Look at your yard flags out there," he pointed to the flags that decorated different areas of our backyard. "They look a little dingy instead of bright and colorful." He glanced my way before instructing, "Tyler, add extra strength Vibrant washing powder to that hardware store list, and we will get those flags looking just like new this weekend."

He's on a roll this morning, I thought to myself, *I need to leave before he adds anything else to my list!* I gave him a thumbs up in acknowledgment of his request before I grabbed my wallet and phone and headed toward the door for work. "You two have a great Friday. See you this evening."

*   *   *   *   *   *   *

Being an early riser, weekends were no different than the weekdays for me. Knowing it would be a couple of hours before everyone would be up, particularly my father, I decided to get a few chores completed prior to having him breathing over my shoulder and giving me directions. Many times, the training from his twenty-year military career, *"Inspect what you expect,"* came in handy, but sometimes it was a real pain. Looking over the chores, I decided I could clean the kitchen and nook area windows before anyone was up.

Just as I finished the very last window pane, I heard a familiar shuffle coming down the hall. "Good morning, Dad"

"Morning," he replied.

"Do you want me to get you a cup of coffee?" I offered.

"Thanks," he said, "that would be good."

He was already sitting in his preferred spot at the table by the time I'd brought him his coffee. As I sipped on my own, I studied him staring intently out the window for the longest time as he let his coffee cool. All of a sudden, he stood up, walked to the window, and surveyed the backyard as his hand reached up to the back of his head to scratch it in confusion.

Returning to his coffee, he glanced up at me with a quizzical expression on his face. "Did it rain last night?"

"No," I replied with interest, "why do you ask?"

"The grass is so green, your utility building looks crisp and clean, and your yard flags are so bright and colorful." He shook his head in awe. "They certainly didn't look that way yesterday morning."

I pondered for several seconds before chuckling slightly. "Dad, I washed the windows this morning. Isn't it interesting how a clean window makes you see more clearly? It's kind of like a positive outlook."

My father's eyes seemed to glaze over as my revelation sunk in. I grinned, and said, "You know, that is what I always tell the children... How you *see* the world is how it is. It just goes to show you at any given time…

*   *   *   *   *   *   *

Your perception creates your reality.

*   *   *   *   *   *   *

* * * * * * *

Be The Change

* * * * * * *

Week Twenty-Five

A calm but strong voice said, "I distinctly remember the very day it occurred to me that there is a whole lot more to the world than *me.* I was in my early twenties and sitting on a park bench across from an extremely busy intersection. I centered myself before putting my complete focus on each person, one at a time, that passed in front of me as they went along; some went straight down the road, others turned down various roads both right and left, and a few strolled past in paces ranging from leisure to vigorous. Each person that passed by had their own life, their own set of circumstances, essentially their own *world.* It was then that I realized that *my* world was not necessarily the same place as *their* world. And *my* world wasn't necessarily anyone else's world but *my own.* Ah, what a revelation."

Clasping his hands together under his chin, Guru Garysheema bowed to the audience that anxiously awaited his teachings from his latest seminar, "How to Change Our World."

"I would like each of you to stand and look at the person to your right." He paused for twenty seconds to allow ample time for the audience to carry out his instructions before continuing. "Good. Now I would like each of you to look at the person to your left." After twenty seconds he said, "Now I would like for you to turn around and look at the person behind you." After another twenty seconds, he said, "Very good. Now please look at me...and you may be seated." The guru motioned downward slightly with both of his hands outstretched. As the audience took their seats, he slowly lowered himself down to sit on center stage.

"Everyone, center yourselves." Closing his eyes, he took a deep breath in, drawing his hands up in a breath-like motion, signaling to everyone in the room to inhale. His hands then pushed away from his body and a collective wind of breath could be heard within the walls of the large auditorium as everyone exhaled.

Guru Garysheema opened his eyes to gaze around the room. "Tell me, regardless if you already know one or all of the people you just looked at, *what* are they thinking. Tell me *why* they are thinking what they are thinking. Tell me exactly *how* they are feeling at this very moment." He paused for a long minute. The audience was so silent a pin drop could've easily been heard in the large space.

"Ah," the guru smiled, "you are all asking me the same question in your mind; *how would I know what he or she is thinking, or why they are thinking it, or even if they are thinking at all?* You are thinking in your mind, *I am not a psychic.* This is good. This is how it should be, so this is how it is. Since we cannot read minds, we must rely on our observations. So then tell me, are the people you have observed happy or sad, healthy or unhealthy, sick or well, calm or anxious, rich or poor?"

Guru Garysheema paused before slowly scanning the audience before him. No one dared to utter a sound. The guru nodded slightly. "Even if you came today with a companion, a friend, or a spouse, you may think or assume you know most or all of this information, but do you really know? Do you really know *why?*" He paused and once again was only met with silence. "Ah, you say you cannot because you are not that person; you have not experienced all that they have experienced, which means you do not perceive or process the way they do. *You* perceive and process in a way that is unique to *you*, because *your* life experiences are unique to *you* as each *person's* life experiences are unique to *them*. All people in this great big world are unique, even identical twins.

"Even if you experience the exact same event as another," he outstretched his palms to the crowd before him, "your experience will be individualized, conditioned, and molded by the paradigms of your existence. All of you of the Christian belief system — consider the gospels of Jesus Christ. They are all slightly different. Even the eyewitness accounts of miracles are not exactly the same. Even now all of you are sitting in this room listening to me speak. You are all hearing the same words, the same message, but you will each take away something different, something unique to you, from this collective experience. Consider world events and listen to the various news outlets — the same event is viewed and reported differently by each of the news outlets."

"So," he continued, "as I sat at the intersection so many years ago, I realized that even though the people were traveling on the same road, they each brought their own personal experience and their own interpretation of their experience with them. I came to understand that we *do not* live in one world, we only *share* one world."

Guru Garysheema clasped his hands together and spoke slowly, "*Your* world is *not my* world, and *my* world is *not your* world. The only time we actually live in the *same* world is when we *intersect* with each other. Our actions, whatever they may be, create reactions that *intersect* with our individual worlds. I repeat again, there is not *one* world, there are *as many worlds as there are people in the world,* which means there are close to *seven billion worlds* on Earth right now."

"Everyone, center yourselves," the guru instructed. "Then take a moment to reflect first internally and then externally. Close your eyes and ponder the words that have been spoken...consider your world... What is important to you? How do you feel?" All that could be heard in the auditorium was quiet breathing.

"Good," the guru spoke softly, "now, everyone, open your eyes and consider the world of the person sitting in front of you, to the right of you, and then to the left of you."

Once again there was total silence. "Did you gain any insights about your world?" asked Guru Garysheema. Several heads nodded within the auditorium. "Now, maybe a more important question, did you gain insights about your neighbors' worlds?" Heads throughout the auditorium were motionless and met the guru with blank stares.

"No," the guru stated with a slight smile. "So, do you see? Every single person has their own world in which they live, and for the most part it is located between their ears and behind their eyes. There is no way that you can understand their world without yours becoming a bias, a comparison, for theirs. Your world will always interfere because what you use to interpret, to understand, to process is in fact *your world.*"

Guru continued, "Everyone, under your seat you will find a pair of World View Goggles. Take them from under the seat, unwrap them, and put them on. When I say so, please press the button on the nose bridge of the glasses. After you have pressed the button, you will begin to see various images in first person — not as an observer but as a *participant.*"

"Some of the many events that you will visualize will be as follows," he explained, "sitting in a house in the middle of a Syrian street that is being bombed, walking in a Manhattan penthouse suite, lying in a hospital bed receiving chemotherapy, and standing to the 'turn the tassel' at a college graduation, among others. Please relax as you complete this exercise. Between each visualization there will be several minutes for each of you to absorb the feeling. Use that time to think. Try to feel what that world is or what your world would be from the visual simulation that you are participating in. Now everyone, take a deep breath, center yourself, please press the button on the nose bridge and now...we begin."

The auditorium lights immediately dimmed and stillness soon waned as the visual experiences were reflected in body language. The guru sat silently observing various emotions played out in heads, necks, arms, torsos, and sometimes even legs.

After an hour, the World View Goggles automatically powered off as the visual presentations ended. Guru Garysheema quietly instructed everyone to remove their goggles and return them under their seat. "So, my good friends, tell me, did you experience the whole range of emotions from fear to joy from sadness to happiness? Did it depend on exactly what setting you were exposed to as to which set of thoughts went through your mind?"

"Tell me," he questioned further, "did your world change depending on exactly what you were visually experiencing? This happened as our Earth was spinning and as the world as we know it stayed constant, but your *individual* world was not the same; in fact, your individual world was ever changing depending on the stimulus that you visually participated in. With that being said, do you now agree that we *do not* live in one world, but we live in worlds *within* a world?"

After pausing for several moments, the guru stood. "So how do you change the world? Well, friends, you cannot. You can only change *your* world. You can only change what you have control over, which is your interpretation of your world. Always remember to be mindful of how you interpret the world because *your interpretation is what your world is.*"

"Knowing this, how can we change the world?" Guru Garysheema asked once more. "We change the world by first changing our individual worlds and, more importantly, our perceptions that affect our individual world, which then reverberates into the collective world." He cupped his hands together in front of him. "We cannot change the world, but we can change another's world by changing our own individual world. It is through change that we can create change — this is essentially 'The Domino Effect.'"

"Think of a tiny drop of water in a pond," he went further to explain. "*You* are the drop of water. Think of how the drop of water then creates a ripple concentrically around itself. That is your perception of your world and that is how your perception of the world affects others' worlds — it is 'The Ripple Effect.'"

"Consider a drop of rain," he continued. "Can it satisfy the thirst of an entire field of corn? No. But consider many drops of rain. Collective drops of rain are so powerful that together they can *create* or *destroy* life. *You* are the drop of rain and how you interpret your world is the drops of rain."

"To change the world, we must actually *change worlds*. The only way to change worlds is to effect the change we want to see in the shared world with our individual world, one drop at a time. Remember, no one can persuade another to change. Each of us guards a gate of change that can only be opened from the inside. We cannot open the gate of another; each of us can only unlock and open our own gate."

"Building a better you is the first step to building a better world or worlds. Remember, as a body each of us are single, but as a soul we are not. There is a limit to what we as individuals can do, but there is no limit to what a universal response might achieve. It is up to us as individuals to do what we can, however little that may be. I leave you with this message, my friends. To change the world each of you must...

* * * * * * *

Be the change you <u>want to see</u>

by <u>changing the way that you see</u>.

* * * * * * *

Sun

Week Twenty-Six

The solar eclipse.

People here and there, near and far, and miles upon miles apart get to glimpse the solar eclipse in totality.

As the day of the solar eclipse rapidly approached, I decided to spend some time researching the event and was pleasantly surprised to learn some interesting facts. Most calendar years, those that have three hundred and sixty-five days, contain two solar eclipses, and the most that can possibly take place in the same calendar year is five. But the main reason they are so special is because it takes almost three hundred and seventy-five years for a total solar eclipse to reoccur in the same location. Of course, that means if one is headed your way and you can get to it, you'd better get there because you won't be able to see it the next time it comes around.

Total solar eclipses are astounding. During the middle of a sunny summer afternoon, the sun, shining at full force, is gradually covered before becoming entirely blocked. The little moon eradicates the light from the great big sun. From the point of view of people on Earth, the moon and the sun align, causing the moon's silhouette to obscure the sun's intensity and allowing the much fainter solar corona to be visible.

The greatest force in our solar system that we know of is entirely blocked out. The sun is the brightest star at the center of our solar system. The sun's effect on Earth has been recognized since prehistoric times, and the sun has even been regarded by some cultures as a god. The rotation of our world, around the sun is the basis for calendars and more importantly the foundation of our understanding of the segmentation that we as humans define as time. Our seasons are formed by the earth's respective position to the sun.

Astronomers and mathematicians theorize the sun is practically 4.6 billion years old and, while considered "middle aged," has pretty much stayed the same over the past four billion years. *Four billion years...* It has also been calculated that the sun will remain stable for an additional five billion years, but of course, who knows this morning what will happen this afternoon...

So, there I was, watching all of these people pour in from far and wide to view this spectacle. Many even booked non-refundable reservations in observation locations several years earlier in anticipation of the event. As the day approached, each of us carved out our little spots and began the count down. Most of us were tracking the path of the solar eclipse on our electronic devices to make the wait a combination of tolerable and exciting. Not to mention to learn a few interesting facts along the way.

As the moon began to pass between the sun and the earth, all protective eyewear was securely fastened on each face before heads tilted towards the heavens to witness this rare occurrence. The actual eclipse in totality for our area lasted only about forty-five seconds, so no one was willing to miss its tiny window. Interestingly enough, some areas along its direct path had a total eclipse for up to two minutes. However, whether it lasted twenty seconds or two minutes, the sun's rays always managed to shine back through.

After removing my protective eye wear, I began to truly absorb and process the entire solar eclipse. *You know,* I thought to myself, *the sun remains constant in the sky. It never goes away. We are always revolving around it. Whether we see it or not due to the clouds or nightfall, it is always there.*

This is very similar to life. Problems come and problems go. Challenges arrive and challenges are conquered. Many times, we cannot see the entire forest because of the individual trees. We often forget that "this too shall pass." The moon's coverage of the sun's intensity during the total solar eclipse proves that...

*   *   *   *   *   *   *

Behind the clouds of anxiety,
rays of hope are always waiting
to shine through.

*   *   *   *   *   *   *

*   *   *   *   *   *   *

Vision

*   *   *   *   *   *   *

Week Twenty-Seven

Well, I knew this day would come. I once had an optometrist friend jokingly tell me, "Yeah, we optometrists put a certain something in the water so when people hit fifty all of a sudden their arms shorten... That sure makes reading interesting." There was no putting it off any longer. It was finally time to head on down to the local drug store to buy a pair, make that pairs, of reading glasses.

My vision had always been excellent. I remembered taking the eye and vision test in early grade school and actually never having to step up to the "blue line" to read, not to mention always being able to read the tiny print at the bottom line. Actually, I'd always found my vision pretty interesting considering the fact that my mother and brother both wore glasses, and my father needed them even though he was too stubborn to actually wear them.

As I drove to the drug store on my personal mission, my thoughts began to wander. *Wow,* I mused to myself, *I'm fifty. Didn't I just graduate from college? Where has the time gone?* A series of images, beginning from the earliest memories to just last week when all the kids were over for Sunday lunch, flashed in my mind's eye, prompting the corners of my mouth to lift in a grin. All of a sudden, I noticed a vehicle zooming into my rearview mirror, following way too close. My hands gripped the steering wheel in irritation. Tailgaters have always managed to get under my skin.

After shooting the driver behind me a hard look in the rearview mirror, I decided to lift my foot off the accelerator to coast into a slower speed. The driver didn't seem to care. Their car only inched closer and closer to mine, transforming my irritation into anger. In an attempt to recover my pleasant mood, I finally pulled over on the side of the road to allow them to pass by. The initial action of pulling over to the shoulder caught their attention, but within two seconds they immediately zoomed on past.

Why am I like this? I asked myself as I maneuvered my car back onto the road to continue my trip. *Why do I let things like this bother me?* I chuckled slightly. *In my earlier days, I would have slowed down to a crawl and if they tried to pass me I would've sped up so they couldn't! I guess I've made some improvement.*

As I stepped into the drug store, I noticed that there were quite a few people standing in the checkout line and that only one of the two registers were in use. *Hopefully by the time I'm ready to check out the line will be gone,* I thought to myself as another customer soon joined the line.

Studying the aisle markers hanging from the ceiling, I spotted the Ear, Eye, Nose, and Throat section – Aisle 5. When I turned the corner to enter the aisle, there was no overlooking the huge display of reading glasses halfway down on the left. After checking a couple different magnification levels, I settled on the +1.1, picked up a set of three, and headed to the register.

My feet froze dead in their tracks as I turned the corner to step out of Aisle 5. *O-M-G!* My eyes widened in disbelief. *The line is twice as long as it was when I came in. Can't they schedule more checkout personnel for the busy times of the day? That's just common sense – "Shift Manager 101."* I groaned inwardly. *I hate waiting. This is worse than the tailgater! There's got to be at least nine people in that line. Oh wait, there's another. Lucky me.*

I forced my feet to carry me forward to snag the eleventh spot in line before someone else got there first. *Why am I so impatient? I mean, it's not like I can do anything to speed up the waiting process, and it's not like I don't need theses glasses.* My eyes dropped down to stare at the glasses. *Well, I do believe I have gotten a little better... A few years ago, I would have put the glasses back and walked out of the store in total disgust vowing never to return.*

On my way home, I happened to notice something up ahead in the not too far off distance, but I just couldn't make out what it was. I squinted in vain. *Hmmm, that's odd,* my eyes remained glued to the object, *I shouldn't have any trouble seeing that far down the road. Oh, don't tell me my far sightedness is going too!* As I approached the object, it finally came into focus. *Well,* I sighed, *I'd probably better schedule an actual eye appointment. I definitely should have been able to tell that was a trash can, let alone my neighbor's trash can, way back down the road.*

As I pulled into my driveway, I continued to eye the fallen trash can on the curb of my neighbor's lawn, as well as the same trash that had littered his driveway for three straight days. The car inched up the drive as I observed the empty cans of cat and dog food serving as decoration for their overgrown yard. Shaking my head, I pressed slightly on the accelerator to speed my entry to the garage.

What a bunch of lazy people! I fumed to myself, forcing my head not to whip back around to gaze in their direction.

Stepping out of the car, I allowed myself one last glance at the trash- ridden driveway. *Why does this bother me so? It exasperates me, but why? It's not like they're throwing trash in my yard. It is how they have chosen to live, so why do I even care? Why does this get under my skin so?* I turned back around. *Well, at least I've gotten some better. Years ago, I would have gone over there and cleaned it up out of irritation.*

I finally realized able-bodied people have to help themselves. I sighed. *Now I just grin and bear it.*

Stepping into the house, I headed to the bathroom to wash my hands. As I dried them off, I glanced up into the mirror to do something I very rarely did. I intently studied my face and stared directly into my own eyes. I hardly ever looked at myself. Sure, I always made sure my hair was decent and that I didn't have anything stuck in between my teeth or anything unsightly in my nose, but I rarely ever really looked at myself.

I stared deep into my own eyes. They were still crisp and clear with absolutely no indication that my near and far sight were waning. *Ah, just face it. My vision is just not what it used to be. You know,* I left my eyes to study my face, *your face changes, not just by age. Standing here concentrating on this person looking back at me is showing me a clear portrait of the past thirty minutes. Boy, this guy is kind of testy this morning.* My thoughts lingered on the few incidences that had irked me since I'd left home that morning.

Interesting, the face staring back at me was full of curiosity, *it didn't bother me at all that I couldn't see as good as I used to; I have pretty much rolled with the aging process as it is inevitable. But the other stuff... wow! In thirty minutes, just look at how aggravated I have become. And all over miniscule events! Yeah, it was annoying, and yeah, pretty much ridiculous, but they were all elements that I had no control over.*

The eyes staring into mine narrowed slightly. *You know, there are people in the world without food or water, and I'm letting myself become annoyed over small stuff. Come on, man, get a grip! I* blew out a soft sigh. *While I've determined today that I've made improvements in certain areas, I'm thinking I need to work on me a whole lot more. Maybe I am my own barrier in some aspects of my life.*

I gave my reflection a final glance before turning off the bathroom light. *Maybe this new vision is a good thing instead of a hindrance. Maybe this was just what I needed to help me reflect on how I see things around me...and it's not just about my eyesight. Maybe my vision is in fact not going because...*

*   *   *   *   *   *   *

The very best sight is <u>insight.</u>

*   *   *   *   *   *   *

* * * * * * *

The Mountain of Change

* * * * * * *

Week Twenty-Eight

There it is! The Mountain of Change. My eyes widen in awe. It's a whole lot bigger than I originally thought, and the closer I become the steeper it looks. I've been talking about climbing this mountain for a long time...but, as they say, "talk is cheap." I guess it's time for action. I eye the mountain in apprehension before deciding to rest at the bottom for just a few minutes; after all, I have been walking for hours.

Searching around the base of the mountain, I soon find a shady spot to rest my tired feet and award myself a siesta before I start to climb. I gaze into the distance while my back presses solidly against the tree. My eyes begin to feel heavy and I can barely hold them open.

All of a sudden, I feel a nudge at my pants pocket. Instinctively jerking to brush it away, my fingertips are greeted by a gentle softness. My eyes snap open to see a wild rabbit nudge me once more. Startled, I can only stare in amazement at this rabbit, seemingly calm, twitching his nose as he stares at me in...curiosity?

"So," the rabbit says, moving his long ears this way and that, "whatcha doing?"

Shaking my head, my eyes blink rapidly. Rabbits don't talk! I must be losing my mind.

"Did you hear me?" He nudges me again, this time hopping on my leg. "Whatcha doing? Or would you rather me say 'What's up, doc?'"

This is unreal. What kind of strange dimension have I teleported into? Looking intently at the rabbit and realizing he's not planning on leaving any time soon, I manage to choke out, "Ah...just sitting here."

"Why are you sitting here..." he chuckles before adding, "Doc?"

"Why do you want to know?" I ask tentatively. This may be an alien rabbit intent on taking over my body for all I know.

"No particular reason," he says as he stands on his hind legs, "just making conversation."

I can't help but laugh...with an added splash of hysterics. The *rabbit* wants to make *conversation.* No one is going to believe this story when I get home. "If you must know, I'm contemplating climbing this mountain."

"It's going to be kind of hard to climb it when you're sitting," the rabbit replies with a nose twitch.

"Yes," I nod. "It will be impossible."

The rabbit leaps off my leg. "Well, I need to be going. Good luck to you." Hopping away, the rabbit stops to call out, "Remember, when there's a hill to climb, waiting will not make it any smaller."

"Thank you, 'Bugs,'" I mutter sarcastically as he hops out of sight.

After rubbing my eyes vigorously, I decide I must be hallucinating... even though I haven't eaten anything wild or smoked any wacky weed. What gives? Calming slightly after rationalizing that exhaustion is to blame, I quiet myself again...only to feel a sharp bop on my head seconds later. What in the world? My hand reaches up to rub the top of my head, and I notice an acorn lying beside me.

"Sorry!" came the call from above.

Did I just hear "sorry" from somewhere up in the tree? All at once, I'm aware of the tiny clicks of something shimmying down the tree... and here lands a frenetic squirrel less than six inches away from my foot. "Did I hit you? If I did, I'm so sorry!" The squirrel continues his explanation in quick bursts. "I lost my grip and it was either me or the acorn. Are you okay?"

"Uh," I begin, attempting to focus on this furry bundle of energy vibrating beside me. "It did hit me, but I'm fine."

"What are you doing?" the squirrel asks, his body jerking here and there in sharp twitching motions.

Here we go again. "I'm thinking about climbing this mountain."

"Thinking is not climbing," the squirrel replies spastically.

"I know," I say, nodding in agreement, "I'm just trying to pick the perfect spot to take the first step."

"There is no perfect spot. You just have to do it." The squirrel leaps back on the tree and begins to climb up. "I've gotta go, but remember, 'the journey of a thousand miles begins with the first step.'"

"Thank you, Confucius," I reply dryly.

This is one of the strangest days of my life. As I continue to sit, baffled by the odd encounters with the rabbit and the squirrel, a turtle eases by me, glancing over at me as he slowly meanders by. The words fly out of my mouth before my mind spurs to life, "If you're racing the rabbit, you are a good ten minutes behind."

The turtle replies, "No race today, but may I ask what you're doing?"

"I'm trying to decide if I'm going to start climbing this mountain today or tomorrow."

The turtle nods and then slowly stops to retract into his shell for a brief minute. When his head pokes back out, he says, "The best time to plant an orchard was ten years ago and the second best time is today."

"Thank you for that nugget of wisdom, oh, slothful one," I sigh.

As he heads toward the brush, I hear, "Better late than never."

Leaning my head back against the tree in an attempt to settle myself again, I immediately hear, "Comfortable?"

My eyes dart around, searching for the source of the inquiry. When I don't see anything, I allow my eyes to close once more.

"Are you comfortable?" I hear again.

Heart pounding, I jump up to closely scrutinize my environment, forcing myself to believe this is all a figment of my imagination. Just as I'm beginning to believe myself, I hear, "I didn't mean for you to get up. I was just checking to see if you were comfortable."

My jaw smacks the ground. Where am I, a fantasy land? A fairytale? Some alternate dimension? This *tree* is *talking* to me. I can't hide the shock on my face as the tree bends over enough to barely graze its leaves upon my face. "What are you doing? Resting?"

"I, uh," I stammer. "I am just...well, I'm trying to decide if I really want to climb this mountain."

"You know," the tree begins, intentionally patting my shoulder with one of its limbs, "the mighty oak begins as a little acorn. Growth must be chosen again and again and again." The oak tree straightened back up in all of its might, and, for the first time that day, I do not have a snarly reply to shoot back. All I can do is stare in awe.

While I continue to gawk at the tree, frozen in place, a sparrow flies from one of its branches to land on my shoulder. Startled, but not overwhelmed given the recent series of events, I turn to the bird. "What are you waiting for?" the bird asks.

"I'm not sure," I answer softly. Taking in the massive sight of the mountain, I say, "That is a big mountain and it will be a long, hard climb to the top."

The sparrow chirps, "Yes, but at the top of the hardest climbs comes the best views." She leaves my shoulder to fly up, up, up...and out of sight.

Jerking, I swipe away the little tickle on my neck and crack my tired eyes open. A little caterpillar is attempting to explore my skin. As I deftly remove it from my neck and set it on the ground, the caterpillar inches towards a smaller tree. Waiting in heightened anticipation, I wonder if it's going to turn and offer me a piece of advice.

When it continues on its way, I laugh out loud, realizing I'd fallen asleep. What crazy dreams...and so lifelike, but now it's time to come back to reality. My eyes size up the Mountain of Change before me. The climb still awaits. I've been working toward this climb for some time ... and now that I'm finally here, what am I doing? *Procrastinating.* Those dreams, my subconscious, showing up as a rabbit, a squirrel, a turtle, a tree, and a sparrow were all sending me the same message. A dream only becomes reality when you wake up, put on your work clothes, and jump into action.

Finally standing, I draw in a deep breath. I am now awake and committed to the climb because...

*   *   *   *   *   *   *

We are what we <u>do</u>, not what we <u>plan</u>.

*   *   *   *   *   *   *

* * * * * * *

Who They Are

* * * * * * *

Week Twenty-Nine

"Hi, Betty," I smiled brightly as she trudged into the breakroom. Betty waved halfheartedly, making a beeline for the coffee carafe for her midmorning pick me up. "How are you today?"

After refilling her mug, she leaned back against the counter. "Well, to tell you the truth, I'm kind of irritated at the moment."

Taking a sip of my own coffee, I replied, "I'm sorry to hear that. I've got about ten more minutes on my break if you need an ear."

"It's my own fault for letting myself get so worked up this morning because I should absolutely know better by now." Sighing loudly, she shook her head in exasperation. "Do you remember Sharee who used to work in our department?"

"Yes," I nodded. "I never worked with her directly, but I do remember her."

"Well, we were good friends before she started working here and remained friends after she left, but, ugh, I have just about had it with her! She has blown me off one time too many." Her voice calmed slightly when she added, "I want to keep being her friend, but I honestly don't think she knows what that word means."

"What's going on? Correct me if I'm wrong, but I remember her as dependable and stable."

Betty's face lifted in agreement. "Oh, at work or any project she's running, she's phenomenal. That's why I just don't understand..." she trailed off. "Okay, here, just listen to this. She'll email me because she wants to catch up and chat over lunch, and then she conveniently tosses in that she's cycling for charity, running for a nonprofit organization, or doing *something* for the betterment of mankind, followed by a link to support her on her $Fund Me$ page."

Betty's lips pressed into a tight line. "Of course, I never hear back from her about the lunch after I've replied and given her dates and times that work for me. And yes," she held up a finger when she saw my mouth begin to open, "I do fund her because the foundations she's involved with do wonderful things. But the fact that she never follows through with her initial invitation baffles me. What in the world?!"

My lips parted to reply, but Betty, barely catching her breath, jumped right back in. "You know, once we actually made a date for lunch. The day before we planned to meet, she says, 'I'll call you tomorrow morning and let you know if it still works for me.'" She chuckled sourly. "Do you think I have ever heard from her? *No!* One time, I asked her and her boyfriend to join Joe and me for dinner, to which she said, 'Great idea! I'll get back with you and set a date when I know our schedule.' That was over ten months ago."

Before I could utter a word, she continued her rant. "That brings us to this morning. Wouldn't you know, the first item waiting for me in my inbox is an email from Sharee saturated with all sorts of sugars and spices, going on and on about us not seeing each other, wondering how I've been, saying how desperately we need to get together..."

Betty swallowed another sip of coffee. "But what does she really want? For me to buy some reverse raffle tickets to help raise funds for her to go on a mission trip to Haiti." Losing steam, she pushed off the counter to sit beside me at the little wooden table. Staring down into her coffee, she muttered, "She's no kind of a friend; she just wants something out of me."

Taking advantage of the opening in the conversation, I prodded gently, "Did you respond?"

She sighed. "Well, no, not yet. I mean, you know, I hate to be ugly because she does do all these amazing things for charity...and Haiti can use all the help it can get." Betty turned her face to mine, disappointment replacing the frustration. "Am I looking at this the wrong way and being too tough on her? What do you think?"

Without missing a beat, I replied...

*   *   *   *   *   *   *

If someone shows you who they are,

<u>believe them</u>.

*   *   *   *   *   *   *

*　　*　　*　　*　　*　　*　　*

Mirror Mirror

*　　*　　*　　*　　*　　*　　*

Week Thirty

"Most of us mirror what the world mirrors to us, so the challenge becomes viewing the events of the world from the 'inside out' instead of being informed about these events from the 'outside in.' Through doing so, you involuntarily ask yourself the following question: are we who *we* tell ourselves we are, or are we who *others* tell us we are? You are the only one who can decide."

Guru Garysheema paused, gazing out at the conference attendees filling the room. "Who are you? Who am I? The answer is simple. We, as human beings, are the sum of our individual choices. We are what we fill ourselves with, which includes our choices, our environment, and our senses. Who we are is a result of decisions and choices we make in our relationship with ourselves, with others, and in response to events either within or outside of our control."

He held up an ornate mirror. "When I look in this mirror, I am reminded of the age old rhyme that goes, 'Mirror, mirror, on the wall, who's the fairest of them all?' The mirror, of course, reflects back the perceived image of the one asking the question, so the one asking the question *is* the 'fairest of them all.' Maybe a better question would be, 'Mirror, mirror, that I see, can you tell who is me?' That is a question that may not be so easily answered by the person we see reflected in the mirror."

"Mirrors take many forms," he continued. "Truly, everyone and everything becomes a mirror as they reflect information about ourselves back to us in some form or fashion. This helps us to understand and actually experience different aspects that makes us who we are. Essentially, every single thing that we come into contact with becomes a mirror whether *it* pays attention to *us* or not. Why? Well, whether we do see or don't see an action or reaction, we receive information about ourselves through what we observe from the mirrors in our daily lives. Amazingly, it is our *perception* of the mirror's action or reaction that tells us very specific information about who we really are."

"How we perceive the personal intersections of each day is how our identity is created and constructed. Further, our perceptions were created by observing previous actions and reactions, and so on and so forth. Even more interesting is that we create our identity based on our perception of how another entity perceives us, which may or may not be accurate or honestly revealed to us by that entity."

"The old 'mirror, mirror on the wall' is so much simpler than the new 'mirror, mirror on the wall,' however, the new rhyme is much more real..." He smiled slowly. "Or is it? Your purpose for today is to discover the answer for yourself."

Guru Garysheema soon instructed everyone to rise from their seats and make an orderly line to enter the Hall of Mirrors. "As you walk through this guided tour, you will see yourself in many shapes and forms. As you approach each mirror, please take several minutes to concentrate on your image while you listen to the thoughts that are being presented. Remember today's purpose: are you who the *mirror* says you are, or are you who *you* say you are? Hopefully when you exit you will have a better understanding of just who you are, if not, possibly who you want to be. Let us begin." The guru waved his hand for the first in line to begin walking through the Hall of Mirrors.

Wow, I thought to myself as I passed through the hall's threshold, *this is a lot to digest. Talk about peeling back the onion. That guru always makes us think, which is why I really like coming to his seminars. He doesn't tell us anything specifically; he just presents and lets us figure it out for ourselves.*

The guru's voice interrupted my thoughts, "Take it from the top and see where it leads your mind."

As I approached the first mirror, I noticed just how elongated my image was. A chuckle immediately sounded in my throat. I was a funny looking dude. A recording of Guru Garysheema began to play.

"Are you as tall as the mirror is reflecting back at you? You see, you must be careful how you think. Your life is shaped by your thoughts. If others say this and that about you, does it necessarily make it so? Just as the reflected elongated image does not make it so. Do you let others tell you who you are instead of telling yourself who you are? Who are you listening to - your own inner voice or someone else's voice? When you look in this mirror, does your inner voice say, 'that is not you,' and if so, do you believe it? Who is whispering in your ears?"

Do I let people tell me who I am? I question myself.

Stepping in front of the next mirror, I noticed just how wide my image was. *Whew! I probably need to start doing some "push backs" to get that under control.* Shaking my head slightly, I looked again. *Wait a minute, my reflection is distorted by the mirror.*

"Does your image look strange to you? Why does your image look distorted? Oh yes, because the mirror you are gazing into is distorted. Does society reflect back to you a distortion of who you are because society is distorted? Who is really distorted — you or society?"

Closing my eyes for a moment, my mind began to race. *You know, that is so right. How many times have I conformed to what society or my environment said I should be, but I didn't agree with? I've never looked at it this way before. I really need to consider the source.*

As my image filled the next mirror, all I saw was a jagged, broken reflection of myself. "There are many, many examples in history where individuals were true to themselves and followed the calling of a higher source. They did not reflect back what society said to them, they stayed true to themselves. Think about this. Whose voice did Jesus listen to? The religious leaders? His followers? Satan? Consider the Buddha. Whose voice did he listen to? The elitists? His followers? Mara, the Tempter? Whose voice did Joan of Arc listen to? If she had listened to her community, the leaders, the church, or the enemy, would she have inspired an entire nation? She lived true to her words, 'I am not afraid, I was born to do this.' Jesus, Buddha, and Joan of Arc chose to remain true to their inner voices, and because of that made a great impact on the world through actions they knew to be right and true, even if it didn't fit into society's norm."

My jaw was on the ground. *The guru is hitting me right between the eyes. How many times have I given up on something by listening to the outside voices instead of my inside voice?*

The next mirror was glamorizing. *Wow, this mirror makes me look like a million bucks!* "Be true to yourself, my friends. Neither be deceived by others or by yourself. Be real. Be you. Be transparent. Do not project something that you are not. Most importantly, see yourself for who you are — the good with the bad — for only when we see ourselves honestly can we continue to accentuate the positive and eliminate the negative." *How many times have I tried to fool myself? Most of the time, I am a realist, but I know for a fact there are times when I see myself not as I truly am. I definitely need to work on that.*

The next mirror was opaque and didn't reflect an image. "When a child is born, the baby is a sponge that absorbs the external stimuli created by the family unit and caregiver. The baby is helpless and is dependent on others for everything — food, shelter, clothing, cleaning, and love. The baby will ultimately be shaped by the positive and negative reinforcement experienced by the senses from its environment. As a child develops, the environments experienced by the child become the potter's hands to the clay. This means the personality of the human becomes a combination of self and their action and reaction to others. The personality mirrors all that it has been exposed to in its own unique style, whether positive or negative."

"This process is an endless cycle that forms preferences, aversions, and instinctual responses to stimuli. Your environment tells you who you are. If you are a conformist, you reflect those qualities. If you are a nonconformist, you reflect those qualities. Who you choose to surround yourself with also tells who you are. Birds of a feather do flock together and serve as a mirror for each other. This tells us that we must know the environment and people we are listening to, and we must ask ourselves is it the environment and people we want to listen to? Or maybe need to listen to? Think about someone seeing you from their perspective; it is possible each of us are more widely known more through other people's eyes than we realize. You must understand that what you see in front of you is how you start, a blank mirror, a clear slate, no reflection. You have become the sum of what your environment and others say you are. Are you in agreement with that? Are you who *you* say you are, or are you who *they* say you are?"

That is a whole lot to digest. My head is so full of thoughts it could burst! What a very hard question... Am I who I say I am? Gee, I actually don't know.

The last mirror was covered with a cloth. "Uncover the mirror and look at the reflection." Reaching out, I gently removed the thin cloth to stare directly into my own eyes. "That is you. Wave to yourself. Smile at yourself. Say to yourself, 'I love you.' Stand up straight. Turn around and view yourself from this side, from that side, and from behind. That is you. You deserve your own love and affection. That is so powerful."

"Are you who you want to be? That is up to you and the person staring back at you in the mirror. It has been said that the greatest possessions are taking full ownership of your mind and to know yourself completely — attributes and flaws. I encourage you to get lost in yourself so that you may end up finding yourself. We look into ourselves to discover something that can only be experienced outside of ourselves. We cannot have one without the other, but each of us decides on the reality of both. Dr. Seuss once wrote, 'Today you are you, that is truer than true. There is no one alive who is you-er than you.' Be yourself. After all, who else is better qualified to be you?"

Wow! How sobering! I thought, continuing to gaze at myself in the mirror. *I've never really just looked at myself. If my life was a film and I could step out of myself and watch the film, is it one that I'd want to see? Is it a film that I would watch the entire way through? Would I give it a standing ovation at the end? Much to ponder.*

As I made my way out of the Hall of Mirrors, I could see there was one final mirror above the exit. It was positioned at an angle to reflect the individual walking out. Words written underneath the mirror read...

*   *   *   *   *   *   *

Be yourself. Be an original.

*   *   *   *   *   *   *

*   *   *   *   *   *   *

Reflection

*   *   *   *   *   *   *

Week Thirty-One

It's unbelievable the effect Guru Garysheema's "Mirror Mirror" presentation has had on me. I've been pondering the lessons for weeks on end. Every time I pass by a mirror, I can't help but contemplate the image it's instantly filled with...me.

Almost everyone owns or uses a mirror. While the uses of a mirror are vast and varied, its function is the same. When we stand in front of a mirror, it shows us an honest reflection of our physical and emotional selves. Sometimes we like it...and sometimes we don't. Sometimes the reflection is met with contentment, pleasure, and satisfaction...and sometimes it is met with disapproval, criticism, and a call to action for change.

Most of us reflect what the world mirrors to us, and we all know the world mirrors *everything* – the good, the bad, the ugly, even the true and the false. Thinking about the guru's seminar, it is evident the challenge is deciding how you will look at the world mirror. Will you choose to view the mirror from the "inside out," and let your rational mind decipher the information logically? Or, will you choose to let the world mirror create your inner beliefs by looking from the "outside in?"

My mind spins rapidly on this question. We live in such an "outside in" world that shifting to "inside out" will take deliberate focus and observation of thought. This huge mental transition will be a work in process and hopefully a work in progress.

Of course, that leads to this question: are we who we tell ourselves we are, or are we who others tell us we are?

Only you can decide based on how you view the reflection in the mirror.

So, who are you? Who am I?

We are the sum of our choices. What we fill ourselves with is what we reflect to the world.

Guru Garysheema discussed the famous rhyme from Disney's *Snow White*, "Mirror, mirror, on the wall, who's the fairest of them all?" The mirror reflected back the image of the one asking the question, then all of a sudden changed to reflect a different image that was not that of the one asking the question. So, there it is. The magic mirror reflected back two images, one perceived and one of reality.

Even though they aren't magical, all mirrors do this every day. My mirror tells me my reality, as well as what others say my reality is. What I see depends on the thoughts I have while I'm staring at it. Now I understand what the guru meant when he said we should change the question to "Mirror, mirror, that I see, can you tell who is me?" Maybe he should also add, "and do I like what I see?"

That is a question that only I can answer based on these questions: "Who am I? Am I who I want to be?"

The guru also stated, "Mirrors take many forms." Truly, everyone and everything becomes a mirror in the fact that they reflect information about ourselves back to us in some form or fashion. This helps us to understand and actually experience different aspects, making us who we are. Essentially, every single thing we come into contact with becomes a mirror whenever we give it our attention. As soon as we give the interaction our attention, our *perception* of the mirror's action or reaction informs our consciousness of very specific information about who we are at that moment. What we do with this information collected by our senses determines exactly who we see in that mirror. We have the power every day to create and recreate ourselves. The mirror, if we can look at it objectively, can be life altering.

Guru Garysheema was so right when he said, "How we perceive the personal intersections of each day is how our identity is created and constructed. Further, our perceptions were created by observation and absorption of previous actions and reactions." Even more interesting is that we create our identity based on our perception of how another entity perceives us, which may or may not be accurate or honestly revealed to us.

I have that onion peeled back. Now I see with clarity that my life is shaped by my thoughts. Knowing this, the questions arise: Am I letting others tell me who I am, or am I telling myself who I am? Who exactly am I listening to? Is it my own voice or someone else's voice? And just as important, are the voices I am listening to positive or negative? Who is whispering in my ears? I must be aware, and when the whisper becomes negative I have to put in ear plugs.

I think about the guru's words of the baby and its development of self, leading me to contemplate my early years. For some reason, I focus on negative thoughts. A controlling abrasive parent, moving around, always the new kid on the block, a little physically immature for my age... You know, one's environment can be pretty mean and can create inferior self talk. Why do I focus on that? Why did I absorb that? Why do I sometimes still see that? It is just as the guru said, "this clay was molded by its environment."

I need to become the sculptor and chip away all of that negativity from the part of me that I don't want to see in the mirror. I have to be the me I want to be, not the me that others and the environment molded me into; well that is, unless I am satisfied with what I see. By reprogramming myself, I will replace existing preferences, aversions, and instinctual responses to stimuli that may not be positive.

The ability to reprogram myself is what Guru Garysheema was driving home in the Hall of Mirrors. The last mirror, after all, was the objective reflection of me. I am influenced by my environment, the people I spend time with, and all that I fill myself with. Choices, it is all about choices, whether they are actions or reactions. It is all about *my* choices. If it is going to be...it is up to me. No matter what, I need to be what I *want* to see.

The guru's words are echoing in my head.

"Will you choose to let your environment and outside influences define you, or will you choose to define yourself through your choice of environment and outside influences?"

"If someone mirrored your thoughts, actions, and reactions, would it be something you are proud of? What will you choose to reflect into the world?"

"Remember, it is not the fault of the mirror if you do not like your reflection. Don't break the mirror if you don't like your reflection. Change what is making the reflection, which will then change the reflection."

I think I will create my own rhyme to live my life by, and I believe Guru Garysheema would like it. This is my starting point to be what I want to see. Every day when I see myself in the mirror I will say...

*   *   *   *   *   *   *

Mirror, mirror reflecting me,

let me be who I wish to see.

*   *   *   *   *   *   *

Mistake

Week Thirty-Two

"Welcome to the Class of Mistakes," read the placard outside of my daughter's seventh grade homeroom class.

"Uh, I'm not sure I like that," I whispered to my wife with a scrunched nose as we followed our daughter into Ms. Wilson's classroom. There were already several parents and children wandering around the classroom for the new school year's Open House, and I could see who I assumed was Ms. Wilson chatting with a parent near the daily schedule board.

We meandered around the classroom, taking in the brightly covered bulletin boards, motivational posters, and the strategically placed learning centers. Our daughter quickly found several of her friends and almost instantly disappeared into thin air, leaving my wife and I alone to finish our self-guided tour.

We soon noticed a small group of parents had clustered around Ms. Wilson, listening intently as she shared some information that we couldn't quite make out from our position in the classroom. My wife nudged my arm, nodding for us to join the group, and I dutifully complied.

Ms. Wilson walked slowly around the classroom with us parents in tow, explaining what each poster within her classroom represented in regards to the Class of Mistakes moniker she used for her classroom. My eyebrows lifted in intrigue.

The first poster was of the inventor Thomas Edison. It read, "As an inventor, Thomas A. Edison made one thousand unsuccessful attempts at inventing the light bulb. When asked how it felt to have failed one thousand times, Mr. Edison responded, "I didn't fail one thousand times. The light bulb was an invention with one thousand steps." I couldn't help but smile. Positioned directly under the poster was a table with a lightbulb screwed into a base with an on/off switch.

Moving to the next poster, we found ourselves staring at the image of Harry Potter and his magic wand. The poster read, "Twelve publishers rejected J.K. Rowling's book about a boy wizard before a small London publishing company picked up *Harry Potter and the Philosopher's Stone*. It is now a world famous success which has resulted in a complete series of novels, several companion books, a movie franchise, and a theme park." My wife glanced at me and nodded. Under the poster in a sealed display case was the complete set of novels in the *Harry Potter* series.

Following Ms. Wilson across the room, we stood in front of the next poster which featured George Washington Carver. It read, "After researching and recommending the peanut as crop rotation for cotton and then experiencing the displeasure of the agricultural community with a crop that could not be sold, Mr. Carver developed over three hundred products that could be made from peanuts." My wife looked at me and I raised my eyebrows approvingly. Under the poster of George Washington Carver was a giant ceramic peanut.

Ms. Wilson then pointed to the far wall with what she said was probably most students' favorite poster. The poster was of Michael Jordan. It read, "I've missed more than nine thousand shots in my career, lost three hundred games, been trusted to take the game winning shot twenty-six times...and missed. I've failed over and over and over again in my life. That is why I succeed." My wife and I smiled at each other. Underneath the poster on a small table rested a display case with a pair of Air Jordan tennis shoes.

Turning to face us, Ms. Wilson explained with a smile, "This is why I call my room the Class of Mistakes. I believe that mistakes are a part of life's menu, so why miss out on any of the meal's courses? Confucius said, 'our greatest glory is not in never falling but in rising every time we fall.' Our children are growing and learning, and with learning comes errors. Learning is also being willing to make mistakes and taking the risk of failure. Many times you have to lose in order to win."

She continued, "Hopefully each of you will reinforce in your homes what I will be teaching here this year. It is my goal each year to inspire, mold, shape, and teach my students to persevere...to keep on going even when they make mistakes, when they fail, when they feel like giving up...and they will because that is the learning process. I believe if you're not making mistakes, you're not doing anything. I encourage them to be 'doers' as I am certain all of you do. Doers make mistakes and that is how they learn and can ultimately succeed. Every day when my students walk out of this classroom, I remind them...

*   *   *   *   *   *   *

Fall down seven times, get up eight.

*   *   *   *   *   *   *

*   *   *   *   *   *   *

Muddy Water

*   *   *   *   *   *   *

Week Thirty-Three

I shut down my computer, slowly pushed my chair under my desk, strolled to the doorway, and allowed myself one last long look at my home away from home for the past fifteen years. Leaving the building keys on the cleaned out desk and walking out the front door for the last time filled me with a combination of anxiety and liberation.

After twenty years in the same career, fifteen of those years with the same company, I had decided to accept my severance package and take an opportunity to make a left turn in my career path, opting to join a new company in a sister industry. I figured it was now or never. *Leaving an old job on Friday and beginning a new job on Monday.* I pulled out of the office parking lot, nodding to myself as my eyes glanced briefly in the rearview mirror. No rest for the weary. *But everyone has always said about me, "he doesn't let the grass grow under his feet."*

The first day at my new job was interesting to say the least. *Let's see, the computer doesn't work, the telephone system keeps malfunctioning, I was assigned a new smartphone after finally mastering my flip phone, which means I don't have a clue about how to operate the gizmo. The copier/scanner/fax machine isn't programmed correctly...or maybe it has so many options that it is operator error... O-M-G, what a mess!*

Of course, it was at this point that the mind took over and brought every single doubt along with it. *Did I make a huge mistake? What were you thinking when you agreed to this? Oh, that's right, you weren't thinking. How could you just throw away a twenty-year career?! I wonder if they will take me back? Would I even want to go back?*

The self-doubt was an endless rampage throughout the few minutes of internal panic which, of course, seemed like forever. All of this was compounded by the old company scrambling to tie up the loose ends that would always arise whenever a tenured employee left, because there was simply no way all of the bases could be completely covered before the exit date. So, I said, "Call me if you need me." And guess what?

They did!

As usual, after a few weeks on the new job things started taking shape; however, everything was still not exactly quite right. There were a lot of elements dangling up in the air, which reminded me of an episode of "The Twilight Zone" or a baseball 'tweener, because that's exactly where I was. Stuck in between. *Maybe I should have taken some time off, gotten away, gone to the beach, done some reflection.* But it was too late for that. I was all in.

One evening on my way home from work, my son called and wanted to know if he could stop by to talk. I told him sure. I was headed home from work and would be ready to discuss whatever was on his mind in about half an hour, which would give me enough time to decompress from the frustrations of the workday. During our brief phone conversation, I didn't ask any details, although I knew something was bothering him. He only asked to talk when he wanted to bounce ideas off of me.

After changing my clothes, I walked into the den to find my son sitting on the couch staring at nothing in particular. When I sat down in the chair beside him, he slowly turned to meet my gaze. "What's up?" I asked.

"Well," he sighed, "I have decided to break up with Courtney."

"Really?" My head titled in a questioning fashion. Courtney had been his significant other for about three years and a fixture in our home and at family gatherings. He'd been very serious about his relationship with her, despite my slight concern and suggestions to take things slow.

"Yeah," his brow furrowed slightly. "It has been coming on for some time, and I think it has gotten to a really good stopping point for the both of us... So, I'm going to go ahead and end it for good. She and I talked about our relationship a lot last night and I think she feels the same as I do. It's just coming to an end. I explained to her why I felt the way I did, and she told me why she acted the way she did. Of course, I still don't get why she acts that way, but that's her...and I have decided that I don't want forty some years of dealing with that behavior. So...it's over."

"Son," I replied, tapping my chin slightly, "I am very sorry to hear it, but better now than if you had married and had to deal with a divorce. I guess I see it as some short term pain creating long term gain." He nodded and his gaze lingered on his hands folded in his lap. I studied him briefly before continuing, "But, I'm thinking that this is not why you want to talk to me, right?"

"Well," he replied, lifting his head. "There's this girl that has just started working in my office, and...I was thinking..." He drew in a short breath. "What do you think about me hanging out with her?"

"Hmm," I let his question roll around in my brain for a few long seconds. "Let me ask a couple of questions. First, is there any kind of a policy regarding dating coworkers? And what does 'hanging out' exactly mean?"

"She is in a totally different department, so, according to the Employee Handbook, dating would be fine, and, you know, 'hanging out,' like maybe going out to eat or to a club...something like that."

My mouth opened slightly to reply but before I could utter a word, a soft call sounded from the kitchen.

"Boys!"

Both of our heads turned to the doorway. Whenever my wife referred to us as "boys," I knew a teaching moment was about to occur. She stepped into the room carrying a glass of water, a spoon, and some potting soil. My eyebrows raised slightly in amusement. She had obviously stopped right in the middle of her indoor potting project to share her insight. My son and I both stared at her attentively.

"I couldn't help but overhear your conversation, and I want the *both* of you to think about this." My face must have betrayed my confusion as to why she was including me, because she nodded at me as in confirmation. "*You* jumped from one job directly into another without any down time." She then nodded at our son. "You are wondering about jumping from one lady friend to another without any down time."

We both shared a knowing glance while straightening up in our chairs. *Mama* had gotten our attention. She held up the glass of water, spooned in the potting soil, and stirred it up.

"Relationships, whether personal or professional," she continued, "create a lot of intermingling, just like this water and soil; it becomes muddy. You just can't start and stop these kinds of thing — you need to let everything settle. What happens if you keep stirring the muddy water?" She paused briefly, just for emphasis, before answering her own question, "It *stays* muddy. Most things, like this, take a little time to settle out, so *take the time*. Remember...

*   *   *   *   *   *   *

Muddy water is best cleared when left alone and given time to settle.

*   *   *   *   *   *   *

*   *   *   *   *   *   *

Fine Print

*   *   *   *   *   *   *

Week Thirty-Four

After grabbing a grocery basket, I meandered through the grocery store until I came upon the Health Food aisle, eager to find some healthy but tasty snacks. After a short weekend splurge of delicious treats, I was committed to purchasing healthier items to eat for the coming week. My steps slowed, enabling me to take in all the products the aisle had to offer, and I soon spied the vast protein bar section. *This will be a great snack for middle of the day,* I thought to myself as I stepped closer. *Filling and healthy.*

I scrutinized the multitude of choices, focusing on the grams of fat, protein, and sugar displayed boldly on each brand. After deciding on the brand "Really Healthy Protein Bar," based mainly on the fact that it only contained one gram of sugar, I began browsing through its various flavors. *This is great!* I thought enthusiastically, *they have some of my favorite flavors. This will make my week of healthy eating easy and enjoyable.*

Since variety is the spice of life, I chose seven different flavored bars — one for each day of the week. *Cookies and cream, birthday cake, peanut butter, vanilla almond, salted caramel, almond coconut, and snickerdoodle. Yum!* The bars plopped one by one into my basket. As I made my way out of the Health Food aisle to continue shopping, my mouth began to water in anticipation as I thought about the delicious flavors each bar had in store for me.

When I arrived home, I began putting the groceries away and decided to place the protein bars with my daily vitamins to ensure that I carried one to work each day. While stacking the bars beside the vitamin bottles in the cabinet, one of the bars happened to fall to the counter face down. As I retrieved the bar to put it with the others, my eyes happened to glance at the Nutrition Facts label. My brow furrowed slightly as my brain quickly registered what I saw. *Hmm, that can't be right.* Raising the bar to my face, I studied the small print of the Nutrition Facts and, sure enough, it was.

The label read, *1G of sugar,* but directly underneath in smaller print read, *15G of sugar alcohol.* My lips pursed. *Maybe that's just for this flavor.* One by one, I grabbed each bar to look at its packaging. The front of each protein bar read in great big eye catching print *1G of sugar* and on the back of each protein bar in small print was *1G of sugar* followed by a number ranging from ten to fifteen grams of sugar alcohol.

Closing the kitchen cabinet, I walked to my computer to research "sugar alcohol." I quickly discovered that sugar alcohol is a chemically altered compound of natural sugar and that the human body is unable to digest most of them. Staring at the screen as I continued to read, my head shook slowly on its own accord. *Basically, this means sugar alcohols are a substitute for sugar that are not "labeled" sugar.*

Well, I sighed as I pushed away from the computer, *so much for my healthy snack. How very interesting that the very item that caught my attention, low sugar, was not as it seemed. How are they able to market a product filled with sugar alcohol as "low sugar?" I guess they are splitting hairs between "natural sugar" and "synthetic sugar," and that sugar doesn't actually mean sugar anymore. How are they seriously calling themselves "Really Healthy?!"*

I headed back into the kitchen and picked up the daily newspaper. Sitting down at the table, I began skimming through the articles and announcements, reading those that held my attention. Out of curiosity, I flipped through the voluminous advertising inserts, and my eyes almost instantly found themselves caught by a great big ad from Furniture Town stating in all caps and bolded letters, *"Everything Must Go – No Offer Too Low!"*

I quickly looked over the inventory selections that were being offered and locked in on the large $299 price over the "Comfort Lazy Man" recliner. *That's a great deal!* Glancing over my shoulder to take in the sight of my badly worn recliner in the den and then heading to the computer to determine my checking account balance online, I decided with a grin, *Time for a new recliner!* I stuffed the Furniture Town sales flyer in my pocket and headed out the door with a skip in my step. *Finally, after twenty years...a new recliner! My wallet will get a little lighter, but my butt will feel a whole lot better!*

As soon as my feet crossed through the threshold of the crowded store, I made a bee-line for the recliners. Pulling the sales circular from my pocket, I began scouring the area for the advertised "Comfort Lazy Man" recliner. After searching through the four rows of recliners, I could not locate a single recliner priced less than $499.00. I mentally scratched my head. *There must be another section.* I walked around the store twice but could not locate any other section of the store with recliners.

Finally catching the eye of a sales associate, I waved him over to me and he immediately came my way. "I'm Robert," he said, extending his hand to shake mine. "How can I help you today?"

"Hello, Robert, my name is Steve," I replied. "I am looking for the 'Comfort Lazy Man' recliner I saw in this morning's sales paper."

"'Comfort Lazy Man' recliner?" Robert's head tilted slightly. "We haven't had a 'Comfort Lazy Man' recliner on the floor in at least six months."

What? Unfolding the sales ad, I held it out to him and pointed to the specific recliner. "This is what I'm looking for."

After gazing at the ad and then lifting his head to look at the recliner inventory on the floor, he snapped his fingers. "Oh, I know!" he motioned for me to follow him as he began striding across the store. "Come this way."

We walked to the very back of the showroom, through the back double doors, and into the shipping and receiving area. Pointing to the back corner, Robert proclaimed, "There it is. That is the recliner you're asking about."

After staring at it for a few long seconds, my gaze shifted to Robert's. Taken aback, I stated, "No, that cannot be the one. That one is damaged. That cannot be right."

"That's it, sir. This is the only 'Comfort Lazy Man' recliner we have in stock."

I pointed to the ad again. "The picture in your ad is for a new recliner."

Robert sighed slightly. "Let me see the ad." I handed him the ad and he held it so I could see it as well. "Look right here. There is an item number right below the image of the recliner, and if you look at that item number at the very bottom of the ad it says *damaged.*"

My jaw tightened in disgust. "Come on, Robert, no one is going to notice that small print, and no one is going to index an ad in a newspaper. This is ridiculous."

"I'm sorry, sir, but that is the recliner and the ad discloses that it is a new but damaged recliner. Is there anything else I can help you with today?" Robert asked as he returned the ad to me.

Shaking my head in disbelief, I began walking toward the showroom to exit the store, "No, thanks."

"Have a good day," Robert called from behind me, "and thank you for coming in."

As I walked out of the store, I realized my ears were hot and actually burning out of frustration. When I got into my car, I cranked it up and just sat, allowing the cool air conditioning to blow on me. My thoughts remained stuck on the false advertisements on the protein bars and the recliner, and I soon remembered my mother's wise words from so long ago.

"Honey," she'd said, "always remember...

*   *   *   *   *   *   *

The <u>big</u> print giveth
and the <u>small</u> print taketh away.

*   *   *   *   *   *   *

*   *   *   *   *   *   *

Purpose

*   *   *   *   *   *   *

Week Thirty-Five

How many books have been written on finding your *purpose* in life? How many words have been spoken about finding your *path* for your *purpose* in this life? How many religions espouse to be the *way* for you to achieve your *purpose* in life? How many *'self help'* gurus claim to have the key that will unlock the answer to the age-old question, 'what is the *purpose* for my life?' How many mediums have been contacted and prayers spoken in an attempt to find the *purpose* of the asker's life?"

Guru Garysheema's eyes wandered around the room before he continued. "The purpose of life transcends every culture, every continent, every ethnicity, every gender. Every single human being at one time or another during their lifetime will ask themselves or others: what is my *purpose* in this life?"

"Do you not find it interesting that the people of the world have been asking this same question for centuries? Do you not find it interesting that there are new books continuing to be written on this topic every year, that new words are continuing to be spoken for inspiration and insight every day, that new religious leaders are continuing to point to their belief system as holding the key, and New Age gurus are continuing to claim enlightenment is the way to discover the answer to this age-old question?"

"Taking this information into account, it is quite obvious that no one is satisfied with the 'answers' set forth or they would not continue asking the question time and time again. It is also quite obvious that *you* are not satisfied, as you would not be sitting here if you were. The search is endless, but the treasure is priceless... And that treasure is *contentment.*"

"The search takes so many different paths. Some choose a physical approach. Some choose a mental approach. Some choose a spiritual approach." He smiled, gazing out at all of us, before saying, "Some choose to use all three."

"Some try to find the treasure within *themselves.* Some try to find it through *the life of another.* Some try to find it by participating in a cause. Some try to find it through acquiring *wealth.* Some try to find it through *fame.* Some try to find it in their *work.* Some try to find it within *family.*" He paused. "Think for a moment, my friends. Reflect on your own lives. How do you try to find this treasure? Where have *you* sought the answers?"

The auditorium was silent for several long seconds, but Guru Garysheema was in no rush to continue and allowed a few long moments for contemplation. After several people shifted in their seats, he smiled and continued. "Many search high and many search low. Many look near and many look far. They explore under rocks and water, in mountains, valleys, woodland, and deserts across the globe east, west, north, and south."

"For years, I too searched for this elusive answer until one day it hit me as plain as the nose on my face. The answer transcends everything in this material world and speaks to the *individual* as well as to the *collective.* You see, we are all connected through our spiritual nature, and thus our individual purpose is also our collective purpose. When we discover this truth, more importantly practice this truth, the world benefits just as the individual benefits."

"As I firmly believe and have spoken of before, there is not one world, but there are as many as eight billion worlds coexisting in one world. The whole cannot be greater than the sum of its parts. If we could each understand that no individual person is special because *everyone is special,* and if we could learn to exert our individual will in concert with the collective will of others..." he clasped his hands together, "then, my friends, our individual purpose will become more apparent to every single one of us."

"Each of us comes into the world to experience, and as we are experiencing our individual worlds within the collective world, the collective world experiences each of us. Ying and Yang, light and dark, action and reaction. One does not exist without the other. It is important for all of us to remember that we are all spiritual beings having a human experience. Each of us has meaning and we bring it to life because we are living. Listen closely to what I am about to tell you." He paused surveying the room before holding his hands out toward us. "This means that you are the meaning and purpose of your life."

"I believe each life has a purpose, for the one and for the all. I believe each day our actions, reactions, and individual decisions should make *our world* and *the world* better. The ripples our actions, reactions, and decisions create should be positive for ourselves and others. Each of us should help the world and let the world help us. We should work hand in hand. So, what is the purpose of life? *You* are, *I* am, and *we* are. I believe if we can make the following statement our mantra, we will understand our purpose in life."

"Everyone reach under your seat and retrieve the slip of paper that has been placed there." Once everyone had their slip of paper and was upright, he laced his fingers together and smiled. "My friends, let us read these words aloud together. In doing so, remember your individual voice makes up the collective voice within this room. Now everyone repeat after me. I will live my life in such a way that...

*   *   *   *   *   *   *

The world is a better place because

I have been in it,

and I am a better person because

I have been in the world.

*   *   *   *   *   *   *

* * * * * * *

Differences

* * * * * * *

Week Thirty-Six

The trip to the zoo had been a great way to spend a sunny spring Saturday. All of the exhibits featured a myriad of impressive animals and were well worth the dull ache spreading slowly through my feet and legs. Even though I was growing tired of walking, my feet and my daughter's persistent hand tugging were taking us to the final exhibit, the grand finale, "The Big Cats!"

During our entire tour, we had seemingly traveled within the same group, two families with children and a few couples, weaving in and around one another to catch a glimpse of the animals in their "natural" habitats. There was, however, one middle-age gentleman who had spent the entire trek around the zoo grounds with his cell phone glued to his ear, giving someone a very lengthy telephonic tour of the zoo. Although he wasn't too loud with his comments, it was blatantly obvious by the groups' body language that everyone was weary of his unsolicited commentary.

At the entrance of the "Big Cats" exhibit was a sign which listed all of the different cats we would see and explained how the exhibits were arranged in a circular fashion allowing guests to easily move from one exhibit to the next.

"Ready, Sweetie?" I leaned over to whisper into my daughter's ear.

"Yes!" she breathed in anticipation.

"We're going to see all of the big cats, one right after the other! Let's try to find what makes each of them special." Her little face turned to meet mine. She was all smiles.

The first exhibit was the tigers, striking with their bold colors and stripes. They were as muscular as they were magnificent. Their stealthy strides through the encased jungle was the perfect combination of strength and poise. Soon, a somewhat bored voice broke through the awe as if conducting an invisible guided tour.

"Tiger, just a big cat."

Continuing the tour, we came upon the most beautiful black creature we had ever seen — the panther. Its sleek coat was shining in breath taking splendor, magnifying its startling white teeth and pink tongue in bold, striking color. Lean muscles bulged slightly as he paced back and forth.

"A panther — just another big cat," came the voice again.

As we continued, a thunderous battle cry filled the air. *ROAR!* My daughter squeezed my hand in a mixture of excitement and hesitation. The exclamation was as deafening as it was bone chilling as we strode through the pampas' enclosure to view the lion pride. What a glorious mane on the lion who the zoo had named Leo. Its large golden head exuded a sense of royalty as it gleamed in the sun. Surveying his sheer size, it was easy to understand why many dubbed the lion "King of the Jungle."

"Yeah, a lion, but, you know, a big cat," we heard from the back.

As we rounded the bend, my daughter squealed, "Look at those spots!" She pointed at the large leopard napping on a large tree branch, which overlooked her domain.

"She must've had a long night," someone mentioned. The leopard continued to sleep soundly, rhythmically flicking her long tail, as we made our way through the exhibit.

"Just another big cat. A leopard. At least the others were doing something. This one's just sleeping," the voice said.

As we continued our trek through "The Big Cat" exhibit, we heard the same comment without fail. *Jaguar — a big cat. Cougar — a big cat. Puma — a big cat. Cheetah — a big cat.* All of these amazing creatures had been narrowed down to "just a big cat" in the eyes of our unwelcomed tour guide.

*   *   *   *   *   *   *

A murmuring began in "The Big Cat" exhibit area after the final member of the group had vanished from sight. Did you all hear that one human?" the tiger growled loudly for all his fellow big cats to hear. "He kept saying we are all alike, "just a big cat." He must not see clearly. I have stripes and none of you do...and my stripes are beautiful."

"I know what you mean," the leopard yawned, lifting her head from her strong paws. "I think my spots are cool, and they don't look anything like your stripes."

"You know, my black coat is stunning," the panther exclaimed. "None of you have my color, and, quite frankly, I don't want stripes or spots. I like my color."

From the back of the exhibit, Leo the lion roared, "And all of you know you wish you had my fantastic hairdo!"

The jaguar, cougar, puma, and cheetah all chimed in agreement that their individuality was what made each of them special. The big cats agreed that humans must not be nearly as intelligent as animals since – animals appreciated and understood their differences.

*   *   *   *   *   *   *

As our tired feet drew us to the zoo exit, finally separating us from "the great commentator," my daughter was quiet. She had been so excited to see "The Big Cat" exhibit, it was strange for her to be deep in thought now. I was pretty sure I knew what was on her mind.

Finally, she glanced up at me. "Dad, why did that man keep saying they were just big cats? Didn't he see their stripes, their spots, their different colors, their mane, their tails, their whiskers, and their sizes? How could the person he was talking to even know which cat he was talking about? He didn't describe what they looked like. If they had never seen any of them before, they wouldn't know what any of them looked like because they're all so different! I mean, yes, they are alike because they're all big cats, but they're also very different."

I thought for a moment before taking a deep breath. "Sweetie, this seems to be a problem we're having in our world today. People think if we point out our obvious differences that we are discriminating. They think if we describe someone's distinct characteristics that they are being profiled. They don't seem to understand that the human mind understands through contrast and differences."

Speaking with wisdom well beyond her age, my daughter replied, "But everybody *is* different — *everybody* is an original. That doesn't make sense because...

*   *   *   *   *   *   *

If we eliminate the differences, we eliminate the very thing that makes each of us <u>unique</u> and <u>special</u>.

*   *   *   *   *   *   *

*   *   *   *   *   *   *

Paradox

*   *   *   *   *   *   *

Week Thirty-Seven

Mrs. Tucker's fourth grade class filed quietly into the Hall of Mythology at the Southeastern Museum of Life and Sciences. The Hall of Mythology had been a favorite exhibit of young and old alike for years and grew each year as more mythological artifacts were procured by the museum. The exhibit included paintings and sculptures of mythical creatures, gods, and goddesses, but the artifacts themselves were not the only treasures found within its walls. The museum also employed very entertaining and knowledgeable curators that brought the Hall of Mythology to life as they shared the stories surrounding the pieces that made up the exhibit.

This year, the Hall of Mythology featured a new discovery of a recently unknown mythological creature from North American Native American heritage. The creature had been discovered in the deep caverns of the Rocky Hill Mountains of North Dakota after an ancient American Indian burial site was exposed through ground surface shifting during the fracking boom. As news of the discovery spread, archaeologists petitioned the National American Indian Council for permission to excavate the burial grounds. The council gave permission to the archaeologists, but required that they leave the skeletal remains undisturbed. The council did approve the removal of artifacts for display in accredited museums belonging to the American Alliance of Museums, but the artifacts would remain the property of the National Congress of American Indians.

As soon as they received approval from the council, the archaeological teams swooped in on the site. After several months of excavation, the archaeologists discovered a statue of a creature which was best described as half angel and half demon. From head to toe, top to bottom, head, face, torso, limbs, hands, and feet reflected what all considered angelic characteristics on one side and demonic characteristics on the other.

After much dialogue and communication within the antiquity community, it was discovered this mythological creature was named Paradox and had been noted in several ancient hieroglyphics and ancient texts. The antiquity and archaeology communities were abuzz with excitement over the relic. Based on their stellar reputation across the nation, the Hall of Mythology of the Southeastern Museum of Life and Sciences was selected as the first stop on the national tour of Paradox. After the relic completed a month-long stay, it would continue its trek across the country.

As Mrs. Tucker's fourth grade class walked in awe through the Hall of Mythology observing all the exhibits, the students were encouraged to quietly discuss the exhibits with their classmates and jot down their questions. At the end of the observation time, they entered one of the adjacent classrooms. A curator came in to discuss any exhibits the students had questions about. The curators at the museum had a wonderful knack of bringing a certain spark of magic to the exhibits through their expressive storytelling ability.

Mr. Larry Daley happily entered the classroom and weaved through the rows of students, asking each child their name and what exhibit they liked best. He was a jovial chap, complete with a sing song voice and a big smile that complimented his white poufy hair and red suspenders. Once he'd finished speaking to the children, he headed to the front of the room.

"It is so good to have you all here today." He smiled, looping his thumbs through the front straps of his suspenders. "I hope you have enjoyed the museum and will come back and bring your parents if they have not seen all that we have to offer. I have gone around the room and mentally noted the exhibits that seem to interest the most of you. If I leave your favorite out, please write me a note and hand it to me on your way out today, and I will send a write up to your teacher before the end of the week so she can share with your class back at school."

Mr. Daley shared stories about all of the normal favorites including Ra and Isis of Egyptian mythology, Thor of Norse mythology, the Dragon Gods of Asian mythology, Shiva and Vishnu of Hindu mythology, Zeus and Mercury and Venus of Greek and Roman mythology, as well as the modern day American folklore of Paul Bunyan, John Henry, and Pecos Bill. He expressively told story after story. All the students could do was stare at him in mystified wonder. He had them eating from the palms of his hands.

At the end of his presentation, one of the students, a red-haired girl named Ella, raised her hand and patiently waited for Larry to call on her. He glanced at the clock on the wall before taking in the young one's expectant expression. He asked Mrs. Tucker if it was okay to take one more question.

Mrs. Tucker nodded her head. "Absolutely. We have plenty of time for one more question."

"Young lady," Larry grinned, turning his attention to Ella and holding his arms out. "You are in luck! What is your question?"

Shyly, she asked, "What about that new exhibit, the Par-a-dox?"

"Oh, I am so glad you asked! The Paradox is our newest exhibit; it will only be here for the rest of the month and then it will be traveling all across the United States for the next year until a final resting place is selected, possibly the Smithsonian Institute. It is a rare find and it is at this time a one of a kind." He paused to chuckle. "Hey, I rhymed! How did you all like that?" Larry beamed as the class giggled.

"Now, the Paradox is a very interesting creature," he continued, "and legend has it a Paradox lived in each Indian tribe and was born half good and half bad or half angel and half devil. The Paradox walked through the village day and night in search of energy to devour; good energy and bad energy. The type of tribal energy the Paradox fed upon caused the creature's good side or bad side to grow. If the good side grew, the Paradox would bestow blessings upon the tribe. If the bad side grew, the Paradox would bestow curses on the tribe. Whether it was positive energy or negative energy, it mattered not to the Paradox. Its hunger for energy was never satisfied."

Larry saw Ella's hand slowly rise from the back of the room. "Yes ma'am, you have a question?"

"How does it grow?" she asked.

"How does what grow, honey?"

"How does either side of the Paradox grow?" Ella softly rephrased. "You said the elders said that they start out the same size, but then one side grows bigger than the other. How does it grow?"

Larry chuckled. "Honey, you are wise beyond your years. What a great question." He could see Ella blushing from her seat in the back of the room. "Tell me, my young friends, what makes each of you grow?"

"Food!"

"Snacks!"

"My mom says vegetables, but they're gross!"

Larry laughed once more. "Yes, food! If the Paradox is half good and half bad, what do you think would make it grow?" He paused, giving the students time to think. "What makes the good side or the bad side grow? Whichever *side* that is *fed*. Does that make sense?"

The once mystified gazes of the fourth grade class were now blank with confusion. "How about if I put it his way," Larry began. "The more positive things you do, the more positive people that are your friends, the more positive movies and TV you watch, the more positive websites you click onto on your computer, the more positive books and magazines you read, *the more positive you will be*."

He shrugged. "On the other hand, the more negative things you do, the more negative friends you have, the more negative movies and TV you watch, the more negative websites you click on your computer, the more negative books and magazines you read, *the more negative you will be*."

"That is what is meant by *feeding*: it is taking in the things that you choose to read with your eyes, listen to with your ears, think about in your thoughts, and more importantly who or what you choose to let into your world." Larry smiled as he took in the light bulbs shining brightly over most of the students' heads. "Mrs. Tucker, do you have anything to add before we close our session?"

"First, students, let's give Mr. Daley a big round of applause. Thank you for such a wonderful presentation!" The classroom erupted in shouts of praises and clapping, prompting Mr. Daley to dramatically bow. After a few moments, Mrs. Tucker silenced the students. "Thank you once again. Your story of the Paradox reminded me of something my parents would say to my brothers and me every so often when we were growing up. They would say be careful of your choices because that is food for your actions. Remember, class...

*   *   *   *   *   *   *

There is good and bad in each of us.

We are whichever we choose to feed.

*   *   *   *   *   *   *

* * * * * * *

Belief and Behavior

* * * * * * *

Week Thirty-Eight

I glanced pointedly at the clock and shouted, "It's 10:35! We've got to go! Church starts in twenty-five minutes."

Without fail, every Sunday morning was a "Chinese fire drill" at our house as we tried to get to the worship service on time. Based solely on the routine frenzy of Sunday mornings, it was a wonder that my wife and children ever made it to work or school on time during the week. After everyone scrambled into the vehicle, we finally pulled out of the driveway and onto the road that would ultimately lead us to our church. All of a sudden, a blur of a brand new white Toyota Camry zoomed around us, even though we were clearly driving a few miles over the speed limit and were in a no passing zone.

What in the world?! I thought to myself in a bought of irritation. *I'd looked both ways before I pulled out of the drive and nothing had been coming either way!*

"Wow, that car is flying," I grumbled to my wife in annoyance. "He must be going at least fifty and this is a thirty-five." She merely patted my leg in an attempt to calm my agitation. I sighed. Irritation was not the way I wanted to prepare myself for a worship service.

Although it continued to speed down the road, I could still make out the Camry ahead of us. My head shook on its own accord when the vehicle did not come to a complete stop at the stop sign at the end of the road. Its brake lights shone just long enough to appear as if it had stopped before bolting through the intersection. It had performed the good old "slow and go," as my father would say.

As we approached the next intersection, which was a few blocks before the church, I noticed the white car up ahead at the four-way stop intersection. The Camry turned in front of all the other cars without waiting for the normal rotation. One of the cars slammed on brakes and blared its horn as the Camry shot past it.

"That person is going to get someone hurt driving like that," I stated loud enough for my soon to be fifteen-year-old to hear. My eyes glanced to the rearview mirror to see him leaning forward, staring in the direction of the Camry with wide eyes.

We turned into the church parking lot and soon began walking up the concrete sidewalk to take us to the steps leading into the sanctuary for worship service. I suddenly become aware of the white Toyota Camry, complete with temporary tags, parked in one of the handicapped parking spots closest to the sanctuary entrance. Stepping closer, I scrutinized the inside of the vehicle. As I suspected, there was no handicapped designation hanging from the rearview mirror.

"Wow," I muttered to my wife. "Check that out. It looks like that wild driver goes to our church. I'm sure glad they didn't run over someone getting here. And, wouldn't you know it, they are illegally parked in a handicapped parking space."

A new usher handed us the printed order of service as we stepped into the foyer of the sanctuary, and as we walked past, I heard him sharing with the other ushers that he had been running late earlier in the morning and was glad his brand new Camry had such great "pick-up."

Umm, I thought to myself, *and how many traffic laws have you broken this morning on your way to handing out bulletins with a great big, "God loves you and so do I" smile on your face?*

During the worship service, one of the Lay leaders gave a Life Application moment on the meaning of a charitable spirit. He spoke at great lengths about having compassion on others, sharing with others from our own personal abundance, and how that translates across the wide spectrum of personal income. He continued on about the blessings of God, particularly financial blessings, and how we should be stewards of what we have. He then said that we are basically tenants of what God has blessed us with and we should be "like a river and let the blessings flow to others" instead of being "a pond in order to keep it all for ourselves."

The more he talked, the more thoughts darted through my mind. *Wait a minute... Doesn't he own a bunch of small finance companies and "pay day" loan centers? Doesn't he lend folks money at exorbitant interest rates, like twenty-five to thirty percent?* I mentally scratched my head.

What am I missing here? He lends money to people that are struggling because they cannot obtain financing from traditional lending sources, and, yes, he provides them with a service, but at what price? Seems to me, unless I am missing something, he actually hurts them financially, as to obtain the loan they have to pay him back three or four times the amount that they would pay a standard lending source! What is Christian about that?! It doesn't match what he's saying. Sure, I realize they call that "risk adjusted financing," but I call it "reverse Robin Hood financing."

I leaned over and whispered in my wife's ear, "Do you really think he should be the one giving this ministry moment?" A pained expression soon settled on her face, providing a nonverbal answer to my question.

After the conclusion of the worship service, we traveled to our favorite buffet restaurant for our customary after church meal. On the drive over, we discussed the morning's message and how it spoke to each of us. This was one of my favorite family times of the week as I was able to understand exactly what my children thought and hear what they heard, which, quite frankly, often taught me as much, if not more, than the preacher's words.

We pulled up to the restaurant to park right beside some fellow parishioners. As we walked in, I noticed the day's buffet special: all children under 12 — half price. *Hey,* I thought with a smile, *good for me. I get a little bonus today.* It just so happened the table we were seated at was directly beside Tim Wright and his family.

Tim was a long-time deacon at the church, and coincidentally, we all sat on the same pew during the worship service that very morning. "We meet again," I said, waving. Everybody smiled and exchanged pleasantries as we got settled at our table.

"That was a great worship service today," Tim said across the table.

I nodded. "Yes, it was." Observing both full tables, I thought about the similarity between Tim's family and mine. We both had three children. Although his were just a little older than ours, they were all about the same size; Tim and his wife both had small frames. His children were fourteen, thirteen, and eleven, while ours were fourteen, eleven, and nine. It was nice that they were all so close in respective ages. They had all spent many an afternoon playing together.

A waitress suddenly appeared at Tim's table, took their drink order, and then asked, "Are we having the buffet today?"

Tim responded, "Yes, and that is *two* adults and *three children's specials.*"

The waitress wrote down the order and smiled. "Help yourselves to the buffet. I will bring your drinks out shortly."

My mind pressed the instant replay button. *Surely I hadn't heard what he'd just said. Three children's special buffet price? That's not right, he only has one child under twelve.* My wife was too busy conversing with the children to hear what Tim had said.

I silently pondered over the events of the morning, struggling to make sense of it all. I had witnessed what I thought to be dedicated followers of Christianity willfully breaking laws established for the safety of others, promoting falsified versions of themselves, and blatantly deceiving for monetary gain...and all of this done before, during, and after the morning worship service of the belief system that teaches against all of these very behaviors. *How do they act Monday through Saturday if this is what they do on Sundays?* I quickly made a mental note to schedule an appointment to converse with our pastor, because I was now stuck on the question...

* * * * * * *

What's so good about <u>belief</u> without <u>behavior</u>?

* * * * * * *

Undies

Week Thirty-Nine

As I watched the debate between the two candidates running for office, I was taken aback by the negative progression of the debate. Not only had their once professional demeanors drastically changed, but they had succumbed to their distaste for one another and were verbally attacking each other as well as their campaigns.

Abraham Lincoln was spot on when he said, "Don't argue with a fool or a passerby won't know the difference." It was true, and I was definitely thinking that both of the candidates were foolish. Here we were in the middle of a supposed professional debate, trying to intelligently discern the position of each candidate, only to have the issues skirted around to transform into a verbal assault on each other and their respective credentials.

The assertions on the issues expounded by each candidate, as I had come to discover by the post-debate "fact check," were basically fabrications, half-truths, or all out lies to discredit their opponent. It was like one of my friends used to say, "those folks will climb a tree to tell a lie."

Strange...absolutely nothing was accomplished by hours of verbal banter — all it really did was work people into unnecessary frenzies, cloud important issues, and misdirect the logical progression of thought necessary to solve the problems of the day. It has been said, "The solution to a problem can be found within the problem." And it has also been said, "If you keep doing what you've been doing, then you will keep getting what you've been getting."

As I turned off the television, it was clear to me that neither of the candidates had ever heard those quotes, nor pondered how they could be adapted to their own lives. They would continue to fight without ever taking a swing at each other. Of course, they'd be doing us a favor if they could take each other out without either of them being elected, if this was their tactic for addressing pertinent issues with the general public.

During the middle of the week, I attended an apologetics seminar featuring presenters from various religious beliefs, during which each expounded support for their belief system. Each presenter took the stage for a ten-minute overview of their belief system to detail the history and virtues of their beliefs. The individual presentations were positive and upbeat, and I found myself in a state of enjoyment as I learned the ins and outs of different religions. Once the last representative finished his presentation, the next sixty minutes consisted of a town hall style meeting featuring all of the presenters on stage answering various questions from the audience in a point- counter point format. Each cleric was given one minute to answer the question from the perspective of their doctrine.

It took no time at all for the point-counter point discussion to become combative. *O-M-G,* I thought to myself, shaking my head in disbelief, *I think they forgot all about the G in their exclamations! That's the entire reason we are all here in this auditorium — to discover how God lives through different religions.*

For the most part, instead of concentrating on the positive aspects of their belief systems to address the practical or theological question that was posed, they attacked the doctrines of the other faiths on stage with slights and derogatory words. It was obvious they were trying to convert or proselytize from the stage. It was evident they believed that to make themselves and their beliefs look better, they had to make the other look worse. It was definitely unflattering, especially once their body language shifted from pious to indignation: a true "Dr. Jekyll and Mr. Hyde" transformation in a matter of minutes. I finally got up out of my seat and left, sick of the negativity they continued to spout. No wonder there was so much violence in the world; supposed "men of faith" were spewing out just as much, maybe more negativity, as the average person off the street.

At the end of the week, I decided to march in a rally bringing attention to the social issues and programs of the day, which ranged from hunger and unemployment to global warming, education, and gender and racial equality. The march was to start at the base of the courthouse steps and end at the Town Commons where several high profile individuals with national prominence were scheduled to speak and "stoke a fire in the grass roots" of the movement that we were starting.

At 9:00 a.m. sharp, hundreds of us began our march. We waved our banners and signs, complete with slogans such as "everyone deserves a hot meal," "equal pay – every day," "$10 million vs. $10.00 – there's a difference," and "all lives matter" as high as our arms would reach. We even broke into a little Congo dance when we hit the halfway point in our march, happy to be a part of the ripple of a wave of change.

All of a sudden, on either side of the street came thunderous boos, hisses, and negative verbal slander. There were many people who were taking exception to our march, our cause to benefit all of mankind. We heard all sorts of phrases against our march.

Go get a job!

Quit living off my dime!

If you think it's hot here wait until you get to Hell!

My eyes were wide in confusion, and I met the confused gazes of several others marching with me who seemed to be sharing my thoughts. *What in the world is going on? Why are these folks so bent out of shape? This is crazy! All we're doing is expressing our opinion and trying to bring attention to issues that are near and dear to our hearts. We're not harming anyone. Why are they so antagonistic? What has happened to the days where people can have intelligent discussions, complete with opposing mindsets, without becoming so emotional and making it so personal?* We made it to the Town Commons and endured the heckling as our program of speakers presented; however, we all glanced over our shoulders from time to time for peace of mind for our own safety.

As I walked to my car, I pondered over the week and specifically how people treated each other, particularly people with differing views or points of view. I thought about how much emotion instead of rationality seemed to take over the discussion of each issue. Each opposing view seemingly needed a mediator since those involved could not self- regulate. It reminded me of what my mother said so many years ago whenever my brother and I argued. She always said...

* * * * * * *

Don't get your underwear in a wad: It solves nothing and leave you with a wedgy and a funny walk.

* * * * * * *

A Voice to Hear

Week Forty

Making my way up the steps to the very back of the lecture hall's stadium style seating, I found an empty desk next to one of my buddies. As I sat down, I reached over and tapped him on the forehead. "How's your head this morning, man? Anything up there?"

"It's too early for anything to be up there," he replied, reaching for his coffee and taking a sip.

"You'd better take a few more swigs because I know the professor is going to start off our Philosophy 101 class with one of his classic questions. Get your brain ready; if it's tired now, it'll be exhausted by the end of the hour." I leaned back in my seat. "I guarantee it."

At that moment, the professor strode into the room, smiled at everyone, and introduced himself. "Good morning, class. I am Professor Dogma, and I will be your instructor for your introductory Philosophy course this semester. I am the department chair of Religious Studies, and it is quite possible that some of you have taken some of my religion courses. Those who have taken my classes before know I strongly encourage and welcome class participation."

He set his bag on the desk at the front of the room before clasping his hands together lightly. "So, without further ado, what is 'philosophy?'" He quickly held up a finger. "But before you answer, ponder first on this question: if a tree falls in a forest and no one is around to hear it, does it make a sound?"

I slapped my buddy's arm and whispered, "What'd I tell you, man?"

In less than the blink of an eye, I heard from the front of the class, "Sir." Instinctively whipping my head in the direction of the sound, I swallowed hard. Yep, the professor was staring straight at me. "Yes, *you*, sir," he continued, "venture an answer to the timeless philosophical question, if a tree falls in a forest and no one is around to hear it, does it make a sound?" He gazed around the room. "Anyone?"

Before I could utter a reply, from across the room came, "Yes!"

"No way," shouted another in the row ahead of me.

"Depends on what you are measuring it with."

"To be considered sound someone has to hear it."

Finally, I opened my mouth with what I considered to be a magnificent answer. "It does to the birds."

A few chuckles sounded among the sea of students, and the professor's eyes bored into mine. After seeing my response was sincere, he nodded and snorted slightly in amusement. "Brilliant! Now I like that. I haven't heard that one before."

"Dude," I leaned over to my buddy with a grin, "I'm brilliant." He only rolled his eyes and reached once more for his coffee.

"Thank you to all who provided input. As you will find true to most things in life, there is no right or wrong answer. Class, this is not a course where you will discover definite answers, but a course to stretch your own thinking because we are studying..." he turned to the large white board and wrote in capital red letters *P-H-I-L-O-S-O-P-H-Y.*

"Philosophy is the study of the fundamental nature of knowledge, reality, and existence, especially when considered as an academic discipline. It includes deduction and reasoning skills. It can also be defined as the search for knowledge and truth, or my favorite, 'thinking about thinking.' Some great philosophers that I am sure you are familiar with include Plato, Aristotle, Sir Isaac

Newton, Henry David Thoreau, and the modern day Thich Nhat Hanh and Neale Donald Walsch. Philosophy asks and then attempts to answer the ageless and timeless question, *Why?*"

"So," he leaned against the desk, "let's explore the philosophical question that I initially posed to you. The question is, if a tree falls in a forest and no one is around to hear it does it make a sound? First, let us consider sound. Sound is defined as vibrations that travel through the air and can be heard. Naturally, we must discover the definition of heard. To hear is to have such perception by means of the auditory sense, which is the function of our ears."

"Based on these two definitions, sound is defined as vibrations that travel through the air that are deciphered by the auditory sense contained within our ears. This means we have to have a source as well as a receiver to create a connection, or what we call *sound.*" He paused, gazing thoughtfully at the class. All of a sudden came a knock at the classroom door. "Ah, a sound." Several members of the class laughed.

Professor Dogma walked across the lecture hall and opened the door. In marched a particularly fine German Shepherd dog followed by a woman loosely holding his red leash. The dog obviously belonged to Professor Dogma by the way he trotted to and alongside him. The professor introduced everyone to his wife and their best friend Cujo — Cuj for short.

"Okay, honey, walk Cuj to the other side of the class. I am going to stand here." Mrs. Dogma and Cuj headed to the wall directly opposite of where Professor Dogma stood and turned to face him. Mrs. Dogma instructed Cuj to sit, which he promptly did, and the professor drew a small whistle from of his pocket. Professor Dogma faced the class and blew the whistle. The shrill pitch of the whistle tore through the otherwise quiet atmosphere of the classroom. Cuj's head tilted slightly. The professor lowered the whistle. "Did any of you hear that?"

"Yes," came the collective response.

"All right," he began, retrieving a second whistle from his pocket. He faced the class once more and blew the whistle. I winced in expectation of sharper pitch, but no sound came. "Did any of you hear that?" he asked. Heads shook side to side. "Let me try one more time," he blew the whistle again. There was nothing.

"What about that time? Anyone?" His question was met with blank faces. "Did anyone notice anything with any of their other senses?"

"Your dog's head moved when you blew the second whistle," someone offered quietly from the front row.

"Ah," he breathed, "did anyone else notice Cuj? I see a few hands, but not many. Everyone, watch Cuj as I blow the whistle a final time."

All eyes were glued to the German Shepherd as the professor blew the whistle. Although no sound was heard, Cuj's head immediately began to tilt side to side while he stared straight at the whistle.

Professor Dogma dropped the whistles back into his pocket. "Could any of you hear the second whistle any of the times that it was blown?" Heads once again shook side to side. "No, but my friend here," he motioned to Cuj, "obviously heard it. So, I ask you, did the first whistle make a sound? Did the second whistle make a sound? Or should I ask instead, do the whistles make a sound to *you*? Don't answer yet, simply ponder."

Motioning for his wife and dog to come his way, Mrs. Dogma and Cuj walked toward the professor. "Thanks, honey," he said, rubbing her shoulder before scratching Cuj on the head. "See you this evening." After closing the door behind them, he strode to the podium and pulled out a bag cell phone from under the podium and placed it on the table in the front of the room.

Wow, my eyebrows flew up my forehead, *that's almost prehistoric.* He then retrieved a flip phone from his pocket and set it on the podium. *The flip phone is definitely an upgrade from "baggy" over there, but still rather old school.* He then surveyed the class before staring directly at me. "My young friend in the back row, do you by chance have a phone with you?" Startled, all I could do was nod stiffly. "Very good! Take it out, if you please, as I have a number that I would like for you to dial."

Digging into my pocket to pull out my phone, I stifled a sigh. *My positioning for anonymity in the classroom will not work with this professor. This is twice he's called on me in one class period and it's only the first day of classes. Ugh, great.*

Professor Dogma wrote a phone number on the white board at the front of the class, explaining that both the flip and bag phones had been programmed with the identical phone number. He glanced my way, nodded his head toward the board, and asked, "Can you make out the number on the white board?"

"Yes, sir," I replied.

"Good. Now, dial the number please." I tapped in the number before pressing the green dial button. After a momentary pause, the old flip phone rang loudly, but the bag phone did not. Professor Dogma smiled. "Thank you, sir. You may put your phone away."

He strode slowly in front of the students. "What did we just witness?" He paused, searching the faces before him, although I personally believed the pause was simply for effect. "One phone received the call while the other did not. And why is that?"

"One was connected and one wasn't?" someone offered quietly. "Exactly," Professor Dogma nodded. "So, if your classmate's phone was the *stimulus* for sound, did it create sound with the flip phone?"

"Yes," came the collective response.

"Did it create sound with the bag phone?"

"No."

"Why is that?" Professor Dogma studied the room for a few long seconds. "We know it created sound, which was proven by the flip phone ringing, so once again I ask, did the bag phone receive sound? And the response should be 'no' because it did not make a sound when it received the stimulus. So...was there sound?"

"All of you are asking yourselves, *What does all of this have to do with if a tree falls in a forest and no one is around to hear it, does it make a sound?* The answer is..." He grinned. "It *does* and it *does not* – it all depends on if there is a *receiver* to pick it up. What the tree falling in the forest always does is make sound waves. Sound...possibly. Sound waves...definitely. It always creates waves that travel through the air. This is proven by both the demonstration of the whistles and the phones. Cuj heard the dog whistle while you did not. The flip phone received the smartphone's signal while that old bag phone did not."

"I believe the philosophical question is not, 'if a tree falls in a forest and no one is around to hear it, does it make a *sound*,' but is actually, 'if a tree falls in a forest and no one is around to hear it, is it *heard?*' We have proven it makes a sound albeit a sound wave. Yes, it makes sound because sound is measured in waves...but is it heard?"

"Class, tell me, all of the voices that make sounds today...do you hear them? How do you hear them? There is a lot of big noise out there." He held up his fingers to list them off. "There are politicians, there are preachers, there are professional athletes, there are entertainers, all with a voice...and the media gives them all a platform. Do you hear them? Should you hear them? If a politician, a preacher, a professional athlete, an entertainer happen to be in the woods all alone and start pontificating about this and about that, do they make sound? Certainly. Everything including their own ears hears their voices, but are they *heard?* Hmm, an interesting notion if I do say so myself."

The entire class seemed to be, like me, mesmerized with this thought. The room was silent. It was pretty amazing for a bunch of twenty-somethings to be dumbfounded. Glancing over to my buddy, it appeared as if his brain had exploded in his skull.

Professor Dogma was making us think and forcing us to think about what we were thinking.

"As you leave class today, please consider and ponder 'if a tree falls in a forest and no one is around to hear it, does it make a sound?' Take it one step further. My friend in the back of the room was actually onto something when he answered earlier, 'the birds do.'" A grin stretched across my face.

"Yeah," I whispered to my buddy, "I do like being the brilliant one."

Professor Dogma continued with his ending remarks, "I completely agree with him, and I believe that thought process leads us further into what the philosophical question is really trying to bring to your attention. For sound to be heard there must be something to receive the sound – remember Cuj, remember the flip phone. Jesus, the greatest philosopher of all, said it best when he stated, 'Ye who have ears let them hear.'"

"Tell me," he outstretched his arms toward us, "the next generation that will run this world...what are you hearing? Who are you receiving sound from? Is it the type of sound you want to receive? Is it positive sound? Is it pleasing to the ear? To the heart? To the soul?"

"If you decide it is not," he continued, "is there a sound made? Absolutely. Is it heard? Well..." his head tilted slightly, "that is up to each of you. That is what *you* decide. All of this noise that is in the world, the greatest of all forests...why is it there? Someone is creating that sound in the so-called forests and they want *you* to receive it. But what is the agenda behind the sound in the forest? And exactly *whose* agenda is it? And maybe most important of all...are you in agreement with the sound in the forest?"

He gazed a final time around the room before continuing quietly, "Are you receiving the sound? Do you want to receive the sound? If not, it will not be heard, and if everyone stops listening to it, it will eventually stop. They believe the squeaky wheel will get the grease, but you can stop listening to that squeaky wheel. Who gives the tree falling in the woods sound? Whoever gives the sound an ear. Who gives the voices in the forest or the world an ear? If you take nothing else away from today's lecture, remember this answer...

* * * * * * *

They don't have a voice
unless you give them an ear.

* * * * * * *

*   *   *   *   *   *   *

Luck

*   *   *   *   *   *   *

Week Forty-One

It was a lazy, rainy Saturday afternoon. I couldn't do anything outside because of the rain and I didn't have any indoor projects to work on. Everyone was gone for the weekend, which meant it was just me and the pup hanging out. *I think I am going to do something that I rarely ever do,* I thought to myself, *just kick back in the old recliner and channel surf until I find something of interest on the tube.*

Turning on the television, I began surfing and finally stopped to watch a little bit of the World Poker tournament. *Man, that one guy has a pile of chips stacked in front of him — he must be on a winning streak!* I watched for a little bit longer, enough to see the man with all the chips rake in even more. Sometimes he bid, sometimes he folded, but the pile of chips continued to grow higher and higher in front of him. Lady Luck was really with that guy. *It certainly looks like there's no way that the gentleman can lose. Let me turn the channel and see what else is on.*

Oh interesting, a 9-ball tournament. I enjoy shooting pool, so this ought to be good. Maybe I can even pick up a pointer or two to help my game. Wow, these guys really know how to position that cue ball! They're not shooting the shot at hand, they're shooting several shots ahead. I need to figure out exactly how they do that. Oh wow, that dude from New York has got it going on! Those shots are unbelievable... He's actually running the rack! Now, that is just luck, pure luck. Holy cow, he actually made the 7 ball jump the 8 ball and knocked the 9 ball in the corner pocket. Luck, plain and simple, pure luck. After tiring of the tournament, I changed the channel.

Hey, some tennis action — I like tennis. Let me look at a little bit of this. Now that British dude is really good; he's got the serve and volley game really going on. The way he charges the net and puts the other player on the defensive each point is the bomb! Oh, I am not believing this! That man has charged the net, was lobbed over, sprinted back to the baseline, and hit the ball for a winner from between his legs and never looked forward! Amazing, but I'm calling luck, plain and simple, luck. With shots like that, there's no way the Britain can lose. Let's see what else is on.

Hmm, this looks interesting. Real Life Spy Stories Declassified. I watched intently as the George Covert story unfolded, sharing with the viewers that he was trapped behind enemy lines during the Vietnam War. He actually climbed a banana tree and covered himself with its leaves as the monkeys climbed on the branches beside him while the enemy marched through the jungle below. If one of those monkeys had gotten curious, Covert would surely have had his cover blown and wouldn't have been able to get back to the front line to warn the U.S. troops of the sneak attack coming from behind them. *Wow, was he sure lucky. All that had to happen was for one of those monkeys to try and swing on the branch that he was hiding on and it would have been all over. Commercial break...let me see what else is playing.*

Since I like history, "Amazing American Success Stories," the incredible story of the first telephone, caught my attention. The show told of how Alexander Graham Bell and his assistant Thomas Watson worked on the premise of metal reeds carrying sound waves. By accident, Thomas Watson plucked one metal reed on the originating end of a wire and Alexander Graham Bell heard the tone of the metal reed on the receiving end of the wire. With that the transmission of sound over wires was born. *What a stroke of luck for Alexander Graham Bell; if it had not have been for Thomas Watson plucking the reed by mistake...* I shook my head and smiled. *Some folks have all the luck.*

As I was preparing to turn the channel, the narrator of the Amazing American Success Stories series began explaining the many years of trial and error that Alexander Graham Bell endured before hearing the sound over the wire. The narrator told how the famous scientist Joseph Henry told Bell that he had the "germ of a great invention" to which Bell replied, "but I don't have the necessary knowledge to complete it." Henry then said, "then get it." The narrator used a modified Thomas Edison quote when describing

Alexander Graham Bell when he said, "success is 1% inspiration and 99% perspiration."

Nodding my head, I turned the channel back to catch the very end of Real Life Spy Stories and discovered that George Covert had trained for many years for that one moment up the tree in the jungle. The story told how part of Covert's annual training consisted of being dropped on a deserted island or in the deserted wilderness and having to survive for a week. My mind started to turn.

Clicking the remote, I caught the tail end of the closing interview with the British tennis player that would now be ranked #1 in the world after his straight set win at the World Tennis Championship tournament. During the post-match interview, he talked about the many grueling years of practice he endured and how at the end of each practice session he would commit five to ten minutes to try and hit seemingly impossible shots from every angle imaginable. My mind spun a little more.

Checking to see if the 9-ball action was still going strong, I had to shake my head in amazement at the trick shooting ability of the man from New York. In between games, they were airing a short segment of the New Yorker at his home in his basement practicing trick shot after trick shot. *Wow, that guy is really good and he is the first guy I have ever seen sweating while shooting pool.* My mind was spinning.

Finally ending where I began, the man that had all of the chips was raising the gold poker chip to signify he'd won the World Poker tournament. The announcer asked him how it felt, and he replied, "My mama would be proud. I started playing Old Maid with her when I was four years old. She started my love of the game."

Turning off the TV, I pushed farther back in my recliner, closed my eyes, and smiled. I'd learned a very important lesson. This lazy afternoon had taught me luck was not about a horseshoe, a rabbit's foot, or a charm. I discovered that...

* * * * * * *

Luck occurs at the crossroads of

<u>opportunity</u> and <u>preparation</u>.

* * * * * * *

Airports

Week Forty-Two

I find airports to be some of the most fascinating places in the world. No matter what airport I arrive at, as soon as I deplane and begin making determined strides through the terminal to locate my next boarding gate, I am always taken by the extreme variety of people I encounter. No one, and I mean no one, looks the same...except for identical twins, but to this day I have never witnessed a pair together in an airport.

Massive waves of people are endlessly coming and going in some form or fashion — some walking, some sitting, some running. Some perched on the escalator as others step around them to speed their journey upwards. Others climb the regular stairs. On the right side of the moving sidewalk some stand while others on the left walk past with increased speed. It doesn't matter how...they are always moving.

The people are tall and short and any height in between. They are old and young with every age in between. They are thin and fat and any size in between. They are black and white with every shade of color in between.

Airport terminals are a clear representative of what makes up the world. Earth is a continuously simmering melting pot of diversity which can be clearly seen within the walls of airports.

I find it so interesting that one place creates such commonality of this diversity. So many people are traveling toward many different destinations and for so many different reasons. Every person who steps into the terminal has their own unique story.

Throughout my observations, I find it interesting that so many different people who are all solely concerned with their own individual agendas have been brought together temporarily by a common goal — to get from point A to point B.

I notice people traveling alone, with a family, or within a group. I see faces that are carefree and faces that are strained and tense. There are also faces that are happy next to faces that are solemn.

As I glimpse over at one of my fellow sojourners reading quietly in the row of chairs near me, I can't help but wonder, *What is your story? Where are you headed? Where are you coming from? What is your own personal journey?*

I view airports as a lonely place, which is a strange concept considering the amount of people congregating within their walls at any given time during every single day. Sure, there are folks that are traveling together and conversing, but overall, even members in a group seem to be focused on their individual agendas, oblivious to the world of the person walking or sitting next to them. This definitely gives meaning to the saying that you can be lonely in a crowd.

I also notice that for the most part, each person is in their own world even though there are thousands in an airport at the same exact time, and hundreds getting on the same plane headed for a destination that will divide in hundreds of different directions.

I believe airports are living proof that the world under our feet is not the same as the world between our ears and behind our eyes. I also believe that an airport is proof that *my* world, *your* world, and *our* world are the same and different at the same time. There are endless worlds within worlds within worlds. *The world is spinning round and round just as my head begins to spin the more I ponder on this.*

So, when does the *meaning* of the word "world" not equal the *definition* of the word "world?" And how can the word "world" refer to only one planet when every person living on and in it experiences their own version of the world? In the English language, certain nouns mean the same in singular and plural form and "world" just happens to be one of them. In my mind...

* * * * * * *

The world is independently exclusive

while collectively inclusive.

* * * * * * *

Garden

Week Forty-Three

I stepped into the community garden area, diligently searching for my assigned plot in order to plant my small garden. *What a neat concept,* I thought to myself as I surveyed the entire area. I could even see some fresh bursts of color which brought a smile to my face. Several years back, the county set aside a couple of acres of land that was plowed and divided into plots for county residents to utilize as a garden. Acquiring a plot was on a "first come, first serve" basis, plots being reserved each January for the calendar year growing season. There were only two requirements to gain access to the community garden: you must be a county resident and garden availability is limited to one plot per family.

Wandering around the plots with my hoe in hand, I soon found #23, freshly plowed and ready to be transformed into rows. As I looked around, I could see some gardeners had been hard at it. There were several garden plots filled with broccoli, cauliflower, cabbages, onions, and peas. By the size of some of the vegetables, it appeared as though there had been some real early birds out here. Of course, if you planned on having a bountiful harvest with cold weather vegetables, it was imperative to get those plants or seeds into the ground early.

Personally, I was more of a late spring and summer vegetable girl and was ready to jumpstart the hope of a plentiful harvest full of tomatoes, peppers, squash, cucumbers, string beans, and butter beans. Scrutinizing the plot, I took my time to contemplate how many rows to make, how far apart to space them, and where each vegetable would grow. I knew from experience that for a garden to be successful, the gardener must be diligent from start to finish. Sometimes it was easy to lose steam midway through the season, but to have a fruitful season you had to stay the course.

Part of that diligence meant keeping the weeds out. The bigger the garden, the more weeds tended to populate. And weeds could grow anywhere, anytime, through almost anything. I had discovered that more weeds meant less harvest because they have a way of intricately choking out the "good stuff."

But what are weeds anyway? I mused to myself. *Simply plant life growing in a place that you don't want it to grow.* I walked the perimeter of the plot. *Sure, I guess I could spray weed killer, but that would defeat the purpose of my gardening, I don't want a bunch of chemicals in my food — I am all about organic. That's why I'm not going to plant any more garden than I want to have to bend over and pull or chop weeds. I'm not going to bite off more than I can chew.*

After stepping off my soon to be garden, I drove stakes in the ground on either end of the plot as a guide for row making. I tied a string from stake to stake to keep the rows straight, then began to work until my six rows were finished. One row was designated for each variety of vegetable. My eyes scoured the plot. *I may add some eggplant and okra later on in the season, so I'll leave a little space at the end of a couple of the four rows that are not filled with beans.*

I quickly walked to my vehicle to retrieve the plants and seeds then headed back to my plot. Making furrows one row at a time, I sowed my string bean and butter bean seeds and then planted the tomato, pepper, cucumber, and squash plants. Taking my time, I made sure all the seeds and root balls of the plants were generously covered with soil. Standing, my gaze wandered over my freshly planted garden. Rain was in the forecast for tomorrow, so my planting was timed perfectly.

*   *   *   *   *   *   *

Several times a week, I stopped by the community garden to check on my plot, to see how the plants were growing and to make sure nothing needed attention. As expected, halfway into the first week I noticed a few weeds popping through the ground here and there. I immediately stooped to pull up the ones growing in the bean rows and chop the ones weaving within the other rows. Looking around, I couldn't help but notice some of the other garden plots seemed to have as many weeds bursting through the ground as sprouted seeds.

*   *   *   *   *   *   *

Time for a little fertilizer! My grin stretched ear to ear as I took in the sight of strong standing beans and noticed that the tomatoes, peppers, squash, and cucumbers were ready to take off too! Before spreading the fertilizer, I gave my garden the once over, traipsing through and removing any and all weeds. *I certainly don't want to fertilize any weeds - just the good stuff,* I chuckled to myself, tugging the last patch of unwanted green from the dirt. Once I finished fertilizing, I glanced over at several other gardens to note they were growing a healthy crop of weeds right alongside their vegetables. *And that is a case in point why you pull out the weeds before fertilizing the plants.*

*   *   *   *   *   *   *

The weather had been a friend this season, to which the garden responded nicely. All of my vegetables produced so much that I had plenty to share with my colleagues at work. I placed them in the break room for anyone who might share my taste for fresh summer vegetables. I even decided to plant some okra and eggplant at the end of my tomato and pepper rows.

As I carried the plants and my hoe to my plot, I couldn't help but take in the sight of the bountiful crop housed within several gardens near mine. *A bountiful harvest of weeds,* I snorted to myself, shaking my head. *Oh my. I certainly hope those weeds don't shoot seeds out and blow my way.* After planting my new crop, I began my leg and back exercise for the day by walking the length of each row and bending over to pull up unwanted green. Although I did this during every visit, over the course of the growing season my ongoing battle with the weeds had become less strenuous. *I guess it's like a lot of things, "a stitch in time saves nine."*

*   *   *   *   *   *   *

My six-year-old daughter was excited to help me pick vegetables in the garden when she got home from school. After we pulled into the community garden parking lot and got out of the car with our baskets, Kelly immediately chirped, "The gardens are sure green, Mommy."

"I know," I responded, leading her through the gate and into the gardening area. "It takes green to grow, honey."

"Where is our garden?" she asked eagerly.

"Right over there." I pointed to our plot, and she skipped ahead in excitement, swinging her basket with each step.

She stopped abruptly as she reached several plots filled with green that reached almost to the top of her head. She glanced at our garden briefly before taking in the sight of the towering green surrounding her. Her small face turned to me. "Wow, there are some really big gardens here. They're a lot bigger than ours."

Reaching her, I leaned down and whispered, "Well, their gardens are bigger...but do you see any vegetables growing?"

She glanced back and forth between the gardens once more before whispering back, "No."

"That's because they're weeds!" I tickled her, prompting her to squeal.

"Do we have weeds too?" I shook my head. "I don't think so." "Why not?"

Bending down next to a full tomato plant, I replied, "Honey, I have come out and worked several times each week ever since I planted the seeds and plants to make sure the weeds stay out. If there are weeds growing, the vegetables can't grow. It's just like when we pick the weeds out of our flower garden at home. If the weeds grow, we can't see the pretty flowers blooming. Do you see all the vegetables that we get to pick and fill our baskets with today?" She nodded, kneeling down beside me. "If the weeds were growing in our garden, we wouldn't be able to pick near as many vegetables."

I continued, "Sometimes I pull them, sometimes I chop them, and sometimes I even miss some. Like that one right there!" I pointed at the small patch of green growing halfway down the row.

"Can I get it?" Kelly asked.

"Absolutely! Pull it out, girl!" I watched as she carefully walked down the row and plucked the weed from the earth. She glanced back to me expectantly. "Good job! Now toss it out of our garden!"

As she flung it out, she asked, "You do this every time?"

"Yes, I look every time I come here for anything growing in our garden that does not need to be here." I motioned for her to return, and I showed her how to carefully pluck each tomato from the plant.

As we worked, my thoughts continued to ponder our conversation about weeds. Knowing object lessons were the best way for little ones to learn, I outstretched my arms. "You know, the gardens out here are just like our lives. We can grow bad feelings or good feelings. We can grow fear or we can grow hope and happiness. We can grow kindness or we can grow selfishness and anger. We can give someone an open hand to help or a closed fist to hurt. Just like weeding the garden, we have to pull the bad stuff out of our lives. It is up to each of us to decide what we will grow."

Kelly gazed at me, and, although she didn't say anything, her eyes told me she was thinking.

I smiled, knowing most of this would need further explanation for her to understand, and gently tugged her ponytail. "You, me, and everyone in the world grow things every single day. Always remember...

* * * * * * *

You are the gardener of your life.

You control the crop you grow.

* * * * * * *

* * * * * * *

Blood Donor

* * * * * * *

Week Forty-Four

It's almost time to go do that porcupine thing, I thought to myself, glancing at the clock on my desktop, *and go see Dracula and his bloodthirsty friends at the local chapter of the American Red Cross.*

As I stood to leave, I grabbed my handy Rapid Pass from the corner of my desk. I had a three o'clock appointment scheduled and did not want to lose my spot. I had been giving blood for years and my greatest fear each visit was not the needles, but receiving the dreaded, "Have a seat and we will be with you in just a moment."

I loved the American Red Cross and the fantastic service it provided, but sometimes they could be as inefficient in regards to time as they were nice...and they were extremely nice. If you ever happened to go to a blood drive and got stuck behind the bottleneck of questionnaire completion before the actual donating, the entire experience was akin to watching paint dry. And God forbid if they ever had to recheck blood pressure, or if all the beds were full, or if a donor giving blood began to feel faint, or if the blood stopped flowing... There had actually been times when I'd gone to donate as a walk-in, but sat too long in the waiting area and quickly morphed into a "walk-out."

Nowadays, I always completed the health questionnaire online, after which I could print out a Rapid Pass. This allowed me to bypass waiting in the office area. I'd also learned to call ahead and schedule an appointment. The questionnaire office could sometimes appear to be the black hole of the donor center. People go in to complete the necessary and mandatory donor forms...and you wonder if they will ever be seen again.

After I walked into the donor center and signed beside my name on the appointment log, I noticed only a few people sitting in the waiting area chairs facing the three offices. I was soon given an adhesive name tag to stick on my shirt. The tag listed my scheduled appointment time. A quick glance at the empty row of chairs in the appointment line assured me that I would be the next person called when one of the three offices became available! *Yes!* I internally cheered as I sat down. *No long waits for me today!* Just then, one of the office doors opened and a donor stepped out, paperwork in hand, and headed toward the actual donation area. The associate motioned for me to come in after she'd seen the time slot on my name tag.

Once I sat down, I immediately pulled out my driver's license and donor card from my wallet and handed them to the associate with my Rapid Pass. While she reviewed my information, I dutifully rolled up my sleeves. I knew the drill; I had been donating blood for years. After she scanned the bar code on my Rapid Pass and verified my identification, she asked me a series of questions, typing in my responses during our required exchange, including if I had ever donated under a different name.

Once she'd submitted my responses, eliciting a *ping* from the computer, she pushed back a little from the computer. As her eyes searched the screen, she smiled slightly.

"Is everything all right?" I inquired.

"Oh yes," she replied, "the system is tracking how many people we process and notifies us in increments of five. You are our twenty-fifth donor so far today."

I nodded, thinking, *That's new... I wonder why? The sign in sheet already gives them that data.* She soon walked around the desk to check my pulse and temperature, pricked my finger to check my iron level, then finally checked my blood pressure. I was the picture of health. She then asked me to silently read the disclosure on donating and sign the authorization form. Gathering my paperwork, she opened the office door and asked me which arm I wanted to use to donate, to which I replied, "Either. Whichever chair is open will be fine — I am an ambidextrous blood donor."

She chuckled as she led me to a chair with a left armrest for donating. As she handed my paperwork to an associate, she whispered something in her ear before turning to face me directly. "Mr. Jones, thank you for coming in today to donate." I smiled and nodded. *Interesting,* I mused, leaning back against the chair to plop my arm on the armrest, *they don't normally express their gratitude before I actually begin giving blood.*

There were two phlebotomists working between the four of us who were donating. Soon one of them, Mary, approached me. She had "stuck" me before — she was good, a real pro, and I was always happy to see her when she was working the floor.

Mary asked me to state my name, date of birth, and home address. After making sure I was not allergic to iodine, she began to prep my arm for the needle's insertion. She taped the tube attached to the needle leading to the collection bag to my upper wrist and commented, "You have hairy arms, so I'll try to keep this as loose as possible."

"Thank you," I replied. "You know, ripping the tape off after donating is the most unpleasant part of the process for me. I'm pleased that in recent years the Red Cross incorporated a gauze tape that doesn't pull the hair nearly as much."

"I completely agree with you," Mary stated, handing me a ball to squeeze as she marked my vein and applied the tourniquet for the blood collection. As usual, she instructed me to lightly squeeze the ball every fifteen seconds as I was donating to ensure good blood flow. My eyes averted to stare at absolutely nothing while she inserted the needle into my vein. *As many times as I have given blood,* I thought,

I have never watched the needle go in... and don't plan to.

After the initial burn, it was off to the races! I had learned through the years to curtail my normal coffee consumption and increase my water intake on donor days to ensure a speedy blood flow from arm to collection bag. During most visits I could donate a pint in less than five minutes. While I squeezed the ball, I became aware that several of the Red Cross staff members glanced my way to intentionally catch my eye and smile. *Not sure what all the smiling is about...*

After close to five minutes I heard a sharp *ding* signaling that the volume of blood in the collection bag had reached a pint. "You can stop, Mr. Jones," Mary said as she headed over to my station, "you're all done." She took the ball from my hand, swiftly withdrew the needle, and pulled off the tape securing the drainage tube.

I held in a grimace. *No matter how much they improve the tape, tape and hair just don't mix.* Mary placed a small piece of gauze on the needle's point of entry on my arm, then asked me to raise my donating arm and maintain pressure on the stick point. A minute passed before she told me to lower it. She cleaned up the iodine residue, stuck a Band-Aid over the vein, and wrapped the bandage with adhesive gauze. Mary then gave me the normal prohibition instructions, requesting that I spend about ten minutes in the canteen area to rehydrate.

Just as I began making my way out of the donation area, I suddenly heard an enormous round of applause behind me. Startled, I whipped around to see all of the Red Cross personnel in what appeared to be the entire donor center beaming and clapping...and it seemed to be for *me.* Puzzled, I glanced at everyone before Mary finally stepped forward and said, "Congratulations, Mr. Jones! You have just donated your 100th pint of blood!"

In unison, they all yelled, "Thank you!"

I was flabbergasted. I knew I had been donating for a long time, but had no idea that I had actually donated one hundred pints of blood! *Let's see,* the numbers began to fly around in my brain, *if my mental math is right...that makes twelve and a half gallons! Wow!* I was pumped! My face stretched into a bright beam as they continued to applaud.

The manager of the donor center strode over, gave me a hug, and then presented me with a T-shirt sporting a big red 100 across the front with a profound statement on the back. My heart swelled with pride as I read...

* * * * * * *

Blessed are those who give

without remembering,

and

Blessed are those who receive

without forgetting.

* * * * * * *

Money and Religion

Week Forty-Five

Good morning class," Professor Dogma said cheerfully as he walked into the lecture hall. "I see we have a full class today. Interestingly enough, this lecture always seems to have the highest attendance by far out of any of the other lectures I present over the semester." He set down his briefcase on the large desk at the front of the lecture hall. "It must be because we are talking about money, more specifically *religion and money*."

A few chuckles could be heard throughout the room as the professor took out a few papers and laid them strategically on the podium. He surveyed the students before him. "Are we ready to start? Strap on your seat belts, grab your note taking materials, laptops, or whatever, and let's begin."

"What exactly *is* money?" he paused for a few long seconds. "Anyone? Come on, just shout it out." He took a breath and repeated his question with more volume than before, "What is money?"

"A dollar!" someone called out.

"What we all want!" came from across the room with a laugh.

"What we all need!" sounded another from back of the class.

Professor Dogma tilted his head. "Money is, plain and simple, a medium of exchange. It takes many forms including, but not limited to, a dollar, a yen, a mark, a pound, a gemstone, a piece of real estate, or any number of tangible or intangible items. The bottom line is that money is what one utilizes in exchange for goods and/or services." The students were furiously recording notes.

"Now, more importantly, what does money represent?" Before anyone could utter a sound, Professor Dogma answered his own question. "Money, the medium of exchange, ultimately is a measurement of value or, more precisely, the priority of value. The more perceived value from either the giver or the receiver, more money — the medium — will be exchanged."

The professor strolled leisurely around the desk to stop a few feet from the first row of students. "We as human beings have developed an object that expresses our individual and collective prioritization of value. This discussion today is not intended to explore the dynamics of money, the economic nuances of money, or the many ways money and value are adjusted, controlled, or manipulated. We are simply establishing the basics, which I repeat is: money is the medium of exchange which ultimately establishes value."

Professor Dogma walked back and forth across the front of the lecture hall. His engaging delivery always kept his class' attention, especially when he paused to either collect his thoughts or for effect; no one really knew except, of course, the professor himself, and he had never revealed the reason for his thoughtful pauses.

"Class, stand up, open your wallet or purse, and take out whatever 'card' you negotiate purchases of goods and services with." The students, some skeptical of the request, complied, and soon the professor was staring at a sea of heads, most of which were angled down to stare at their debit, credit, or university spending cards. Once he was satisfied, Professor Dogma continued his gait.

"If each of you were to give me several months of statements that itemized your individual transactions, I could tell what your priorities are. I could determine your interests. I could pinpoint what's important to you by how you use your money and what takes priority in your daily lives. *How,* you ask? Simply by analyzing the way you spend your money. Remember, when it is all said and done, it always comes back to money. Why? The answer to that question is plain and simple: it is money that measures priority. Please be seated. You may return your cards to your purse or wallet."

Once everyone had returned to their seats, the professor continued, "You are asking yourself, *What does all of this talk of money have to do with religion?* Quite a lot, actually. Consider all the ancient temples – what were they *made* with and what were they *filled* with?" Professor Dogma held out his hands as he waited for a reply.

"Treasure," a voice called out.

The professor pointed in the direction of the voice. "That's right! The treasures of their day. 'Treasures' translates into the modern word 'money.' Consider religions across the world – what do they instruct? 'Bring your first fruits or money to the *holy place,*' which is another word for temple or church. Consider how organized religions function. A few followers of a specific teaching or doctrine form a group and that group begins meeting regularly. In order to continue their regular meetings, what do they do?"

"Send around the collection plate," one student stated dryly.

"You must be Baptist," laughed the professor, "but you are exactly right. They collect money from the individuals in the group to perpetuate the group. The group then begins recruiting new individuals to join their group and, you got it, solicits them for support to continue the growth of their band of merry followers. Do you see where I am going with this?" Slight tension had formed among the group of students before him. Some were staring with widened eyes, others projected a glow of irritation, and some nodded enthusiastically.

"Think about this," he continued, leaning back against the desk, "the doctrinal teachings of religion are to give your value, represented by money, to God or whatever supreme being is worshipped. This doctrine has been transferred to the religion or belief system, which through transference makes the religious body or group stand for God. Are you following me?" his gaze traveled over the stadium-like seating.

"For all practical purposes, if you are giving to the religion, in your mind you are giving to God. Guess what happened next in the evolution of religion? Belief systems began spreading out all over geographically and the new groups would solicit from their members to perpetuate the local group, then a portion of the local money would go to the parent group," he snorted in amusement. "This type of system would make Bernie Madoff proud." After being met with mostly blank stares, he went further to explain, "You know, the very original Ponzi scheme was modeled after the Church — as long as you get new members and they contribute, your group keeps growing and the pockets of the parent group continues to grow."

He took in the conflicting expressions of the audience before him. "As expected, I see many of you out there shaking your heads in disagreement with my analysis. Each of you that do not agree with me, consider these facts: the Catholic Church is the third largest landowner in the world, the Mormon religion holds assets approaching forty billion dollars, the Hindu Padmanabhaswamy holds assets of twenty- two billion dollars, and the Church of Scientology has a mere one billion dollars of assets. Whoever said religion doesn't pay is utterly wrong. It pays and it pays big."

He pushed off of the desk to resume pacing in front of the students. "Consider how western religion has morphed in this generation. Instead of mainstream denominations that have been around for centuries, we now see independent churches springing up everywhere. These independent churches own media outlets, retreat centers, and even coliseums. A while back, one out in California even owned a crystal cathedral; of course, they ended up filing bankruptcy and were bought by the eight hundred pound gorilla named *the Catholic Church.* And why is it that the original crystal cathedral ministry failed? Because of dwindling membership, they couldn't keep the Ponzi scheme alive."

"You say I am cynical," he stated thoughtfully after a few long seconds of silence. "I say I am a realist. Consider now the televangelists. Have you noticed many of them own private jets, million dollar-plus homes, their own publishing companies, receive favorable income tax treatment, and almost always end their broadcast with a plea for, you got it, money? Now, the money they plea for is a donation to God, and the work and vision of their religion is inspired by God. But if you start looking beyond all of that, it seems as if they themselves are personally benefitting in proportion with the success of their ministry and also in proportion with the donations they receive... Interesting, wouldn't you agree?"

"So, where does all of this lead us to?" Professor Dogma studied the room. "I for one was a faithful follower of a certain sect and for years faithfully gave of my first fruits — money — to my chosen belief system, to my church. I also helped manage this church's money, serving as their treasurer for many, many years. I developed and presented budgets for the members to discuss and approve. The more I managed the money aspect of the church, the more I questioned exactly where the money was going."

"All of you are asking now, *What do you mean?*" He folded his arms across his chest. "Well, I began to notice that out of every dollar that was collected for God about *seventy cents* was utilized for the compensation for the church staff and for the upkeep of the building and grounds that our church worshipped in. This meant that only *thirty cents* of every dollar was actually put toward the very thing that the money was being collected for to start off with...*God*. *God* was not receiving the first fruits, *God* was receiving the leftovers." He paused to take in the various expressions in the room. "I will say out loud what I know this young lady in the third row is thinking – unbelievable!" Several students laughed while others were frozen in shock and disgust.

"So, here is what I say," his fingers laced together. "Just like an individual, if you want to find out what the priority of a religion or church or belief system is...*follow the money*. I encourage each of you to ask of your belief system, your religion, your church the following: Is the money being used in an effort to make this a better world and to help those in need, or is the money just being utilized to perpetuate itself instead of perpetuating that which it purportedly stands for?

Is the money being used for more buildings, more salaries, more enhancements for the church itself? The church will tell you that the church *has* to spend the money on themselves to be able to continue to teach about and grow the kingdom of God."

Professor Dogma stepped forward. "But I say this in rebuttal. If it is true that the only way anyone can see the Spirit of God is through the *actions* and *attitudes* of another human, then shouldn't what we *do* and say show all the humans within our circle of influence what we believe in and who our God is?" He regarded each face in the room thoughtfully. "You know, Jesus the Christ said, 'Lay not up for yourselves treasures upon earth where moth and rust doth corrupt and thieves break in and steal.'"

Professor Dogma stared out into the audience of students for several long seconds, allowing the message he had delivered to sink in, before continuing softly, "I believe you will be shocked when you break down every dollar contributed to your religion, your church, and follow exactly where it goes and what it is used for. It has been said the truth will set you free... I say follow the money and you will find the truth. I find it so interesting that as recorded in the gospels of the Holy Bible, the Christ spoke of money more than anything else because he knew that money represented priorities. I believe he said it best when he stated...

* * * * * * *

For where your treasure is so there will be your heart.

* * * * * * *

Making a Difference

Week Forty-Six

As I pull into the grocery store parking lot, I deftly maneuver around a shopping cart that is obviously stranded. *It's a good thing I saw it before I made my turn into that parking space,* I shook my head in annoyance. *My car would have collected one more battle scar to reduce the old trade-in value.* Once I park in an open parking spot, I leave my car to briskly stride to the abandoned cart, grab it, and push it swiftly into the opened arms of the cart return area.

Man, I don't have time for this today. I'm really pushing it to make it to work on time as it is now! Can't people put their own carts away? I just don't get it. It only takes an extra couple of seconds. Maybe they didn't have a couple of seconds...I know I don't have a couple of seconds right now, but here I am using them anyway.

My head shakes side to side in disbelief while I make my way through the littered parking lot. *Trash here, trash there, trash is everywhere!* My eyes roam the parking lot until I spot not one, not two, but four different trash cans in easy to access locations. I begin to stoop down and snatch up trash as I head to the front entrance of the store. *I certainly can't clean the whole parking lot,* I think to myself while stuffing the trash into the trash bin right outside the entrance. *But I can pick up what I can along the way.*

Making quick work of my short grocery list, I speed up and down the aisles and finally to the checkout register. Just as I put my basket on the belt, I notice another customer walking hurriedly to the same checkout lane. She only has one item in her hand and a pained expression colors her face once she realizes I'll be in front of her.

As she settles in restlessly behind me, I turn and smile, motioning for her to go ahead of me. Curiosity and surprise replace the dread on her face, and she asks, "Are you sure?"

"Absolutely," I nod. "You only have one item. Please, go ahead."

The tenseness stiffening her body softens. "Oh, thank you so much!" She skirts around me and places her item on the belt. "I'm already running a little late, so this is amazing. Thank you!"

I nod again, grimacing inwardly at my own predicament as I listen to the *tick-tock* reverberate through my head as the internal clock inches closer to 8:00.

*　　*　　*　　*　　*　　*　　*

Turning into the corporate parking lot, I zoom into the first parking spot I see. I hurriedly pull the keys from the ignition and jump out of my car, sprinting to the employee entrance of my office building. Looking at the clock right above the entry way, I note that I have seven minutes to get some coffee, hit the restroom, and make it to my cubicle to clock in before getting docked fifteen minutes of pay. Flinging the door open, and very thankful no one was behind me so I didn't have to hold it open for them, I rush inside.

Once in the break room, I grab a clean coffee cup from the drying rack and quickly pour myself a cup of coffee, careful not to slosh it everywhere in my haste, until the last drop of coffee from the pot plops into my cup. *Crap,* I huff to myself, *I got the last cup! I can't leave the pot empty! Argh, I don't have time for this!* I quickly remove the old filter, throw it in the trash can, grab a new filter and coffee packet from the supply drawer, stuff the filter in the reservoir, rip open the coffee packet and pour it into the filtered reservoir, shove the reservoir into place, and hit the brew button. *Less than twenty seconds! That must be a world record for this machine.*

Setting my coffee cup on the break room table, I head to the restroom for a much needed pit stop. As soon I finish with the call of nature, I reach for some toilet paper and unroll the last little bit of tissue. I groan in frustration. *I've got to go, but I can't just leave an empty roll here. I mean, I guess I could, but no, no, I can't do that. If it was me who came in next and realized there was no toilet paper just when I was finishing up and had to jump up off the seat and bunny hop over to the supply cabinet to get some more, I'd be extremely frustrated.*

I immediately spin to grab a new roll of toilet paper, tear it open, pull the old roll off, and slip the new roll on. Rapidly washing my hands, I stare into the mirror and shake my head. *What a morning.* I leave the restroom to step back into the break room to grab my coffee. Glancing up at the clock, my stomach lurches. *Crap...it's 8:01. Man, that bites. Well, I might as well just take my time now. Whether I make it to my desk at 8:02 or 8:14, I still get docked fifteen minutes pay.*

Strolling down the hall in irritation over what caused me to be late, something white on the floor catches my eye. Stooping down to pick it up, I notice it's a page from a book, more specifically a devotional. After scanning its contents, I can't help but smile to myself. *I believe they call this synchronicity.*

The title to this devotion was "Nobody Need Wait a Single Moment Before Starting to Improve the World." The devotion began by asking the reader to seize the opportunities that come their way each day to make a difference. It went on to say that many times we think making a difference in the world must be some kind of monumental or earth shattering event to impact hundreds or thousands. It read that making a difference doesn't have to be something big because it is all about recognizing the moment. It can be anything that creates a positive M-O-M, *moment of magic,* instead of a negative M-O-M, *moment of misery.*

Hmmm, I actually did that today! I think in satisfaction. *I possibly saved a dent in someone's car, slightly reduced the parking lot's litter decoration, reduced stress for another shopper, thought of the next person coming through for a cup of coffee, and was considerate of the next person's appointed time with Charmin. I did do it! I actually seized many moments.*

The devotion went on to challenge its readers to capture the moments in each day to make someone smile or laugh, and to be a *stepping stone* instead of a *stumbling block*. It concluded by stating the greatest gift anyone can give another is their attention. I smile, all irritation leaving my body. Honestly, I'm proud of myself, even though I did growl several times as I was seizing the moments I encountered on my way to work this morning.

The moral of this devotion is so great, I'm going to tape it in my cubicle so I can look at it every day. It reads...

*   *   *   *   *   *   *

Making a difference only takes one thing: YOU.

*   *   *   *   *   *   *

* * * * * * *

Flower Power

* * * * * * *

Week Forty-Seven

I am flittering, floating, and falling through the air. What a strange feeling to be weightless... free falling...and now plummeting in a downward spiral! *Thump!* Ouch! That was hard. Huh, there's a little bit of a cushion here now... Soft, maybe a little grainy and –

Ah! What's that? I'm being pelted by something. Oh, I'm suffocating... I can't move... Hey, I'm covered with the same stuff I landed on. Nowhere to go... I'm stuck! But it's also kind of cozy. Well... maybe I'll just sleep for now.

* * * * * * *

Everywhere around me is cold, hard, and dark. I can't see anything, but I really want to wiggle around and bust out of here to explore. I'm not sure why I can't. It's so frustrating. I'm stuck in the darkness! I want to stretch, to grow, to be *free!* I am tired of the cold and hard. Maybe I can move soon. Maybe I can break through whatever is pinning me down.

Maybe I will soon be free.

* * * * * * *

It's finally getting warmer! It's not cold, but cool and just a little wet. Hmm, maybe moist is more accurate. I can tell I'm a little softer around the edges. I am able to move a little, and I think I'm about to grow. It feels good not to be so confined in such a tight space.

* * * * * * *

The earth around me emits a pleasant warmth as I continue to feel softer. The layers of my shells are cracking and I know I'll be busting out of it soon! I am pushing and stretching. Out, I want out! It's just a matter of time now.

*   *   *   *   *   *   *

One final push and – *POP!* Finally, I am through! Woohoo, I have broken out and am breaking out every which a way! It feels so good to stretch out after all that time cooped up in that tiny shell. What a relief!

Huh, it sure is dark in here. At least the dirt isn't as hard as my shell was. Hey, I can see others breaking free of their shells all around me. Hey guys! We did it!

I am growing, stretching, and reaching all the time. My gaze is focused upward even though I'm sprouting up, down, and out. I can feel myself sifting through the dirt. Just like me, all of my friends are stretching out rapidly. We are all making strides in our underground race, competing with each other as we spread ourselves far and wide.

*   *   *   *   *   *   *

Today I feel as though I am stronger than ever! I persevere, pushing forward, and make a lot more headway through the dirt than before. I am lifting up higher and stretching down lower.

One more surge upward and the pressure lessens until it feels almost nonexistent...like I am about to push all the way through the remaining dirt. I can see it's getting lighter and the dirt around me looks brown for once. One more final reach and, all of a sudden...

I am at ground zero.

I did it! Joy fills me from top to bottom. I have burst through! I sway in the slight breeze, relishing the cool air. The sky is a brilliant blue and I am surrounded no longer by darkness, but a sea of green.

I have arrived.

Free! I am finally free! No more confines of my seed home. No more pressure from the weight of dirt on top of me. I am strong! I am alive! I am smiling!

Taking in my new home, I see there are a whole lot of pale green stems popping through the ground, complete with tiny dirt hats on their heads. There are a bunch of us, and we continue to reach higher, attempting to grow taller with each passing second.

*   *   *   *   *   *   *

The sun warms me and the rain quenches my thirst. I grow stronger each day. Sometimes it's chilly at night, but my strength is not broken. I simply shiver through it with my friends, clinging to the hope of the new day filled with golden rays of warmth.

Every so often, a butterfly, a dragonfly, a bee, or a bug hovers overhead just to take a look see. As I gaze around the sea of green, standing straight and proud, I know many eyes are waiting for our transformation into the waves of color we are destined to become.

*   *   *   *   *   *   *

Waking up today, I feel a little different and I see that my leaves have finally sprouted up and out. I wiggle them at my buddies in a wave. It's beginning to get a little crowded in the bed, but all of us are working in concert to grow our individual beauty for all to see.

*   *   *   *   *   *   *

Finally, I am weighted with a bud and so are others. Oh, this will surely be a sight to see! Catching a glimpse of my friends, I see they are as parched as I am. We could all use a long drink of water. It has been a little dry lately. The sun is hot and the spring breeze has stolen some of our moisture. Although no one is complaining, a little water to quench this thirst, possibly from the heavy cloud in the distance, would be perfect for our future blooms.

Buzz! All of our insect friends are working diligently in our flower community. They are zooming from one flower to the next, bringing our blooms to life with their magical massage. It will not be long now. My petals are aching to open, as are my friends'. We can barely make out the hint of each other's unique colors. We are full of anticipation, knowing we are going to bust out in vibrant bursts!

*   *   *   *   *   *   *

Wow! How wonderful! We are a sight to see! As I gaze around in awe, I take in all the beauty from our kaleidoscope of color. The faces of those strolling by to see us are almost as beautiful. We enjoy their smiles and their appreciation of the fact that all of us have come to bring brightness and color to wherever we are planted. We all enjoy the positive Feng shui we create. There is nothing quite like us – continuously cheerful, full of life, playing our own individual parts within the whole to brighten the landscape for all whose paths we intersect. We don't compete with each other. We know we are unique — we all have different colors, heights, and petals. We simply bloom where we are planted.

Don't you want to join us? Don't you want to bring smiles to all along your way? How can you be like a flower every day? It is simple really, just remember to...

*   *   *   *   *   *   *

Live each of your days in full bloom.

*   *   *   *   *   *   *

* * * * * * *

Present

* * * * * * *

Week Forty-Eight

Adams?"

"Here."

"Allen?"

"Here."

"Arnold?"

"Right here."

"Berry?"

"Present."

"Brown? Brown... M. Brown..."

Oh crap! I thought in a sudden jolt of awareness. *That's me! Raise your hand, dummy. You don't need to be counted absent when you're in the room!* Shaking the cobwebs out of my head, I halfway raised my hand into the air. "Sorry," I blurted out. "I'm present."

My professor eyed me, assessing my intentions, before lowering his gaze back to the endless list of names before him. Most of our professors passed around a sheet for us to sign or had us initial by our names, but this particular professor was old school. He called out the roll for every student in every class. The monotonous tone of his voice reminded me of the teacher in the 1980's movie, "Ferris Bueller's Day Off." And at eight o'clock in the morning, it was enough to put anyone right back to sleep.

As I listened to the professor go on and on, I found myself pondering the student responses he received. It was a simple unspoken question he asked. *Are you in this room for this specific class?* Most said a variation of *here,* some said *present,* one guy even elicited some chuckles when he replied, "Yo."

My mind circled around the word "present." Drifting back to just minutes earlier, I reflected on my response. I had answered present... but was *I* really? Yes, in a sense. I was physically in this seat so my response was correct. But was I really present? My mind had been a million miles away when the professor called my name, and it took three attempts before it registered he was speaking to me and before I snapped back to the present...well, the present situation. So, what does being present actually mean?

In my art appreciation class, a quote from Leonardo Da Vinci was printed on the top of the class syllabus that was passed out on our first day of class. The quote read, "The average human being looks without seeing, listens without hearing, touches without feeling, eats without tasting, moves without physical awareness, inhales without awareness of odor or fragrance, and talks without thinking."

While I didn't agree with all of the great Da Vinci's observations, I found that particular statement to be mostly true based on my own observations in life. Many times, items, events, and people passed before our eyes and we simply didn't take notice unless they were particularly shocking. It was the everyday, the ordinary, the normal daily events we didn't focus on. We needed to be present in each day of our life.

Yeah, I nodded in agreement with myself, *like when I go to Mom and Dad's house... Unless things are in total disarray, I don't notice if something's different or out of place. I mean, I'm not O.C.D or anything. Ha, and what about with Joe? Geez, he's my buddy and all, but sometimes he talks so much, I can see his mouth moving but not hear a word he's saying because I've turned my focus elsewhere. Our skin is our largest sensory preceptor, and most of the time I don't even physically feel things unless I become uncomfortable or if it's a new sensation. And sometimes I'm in such a rush between classes, I'll gulp down my food without really even tasting it. Eh, the smelling part is a stretch. Most smells, pleasant and unpleasant, aren't usually overlooked. But talking without thinking...foot/mouth disorder? Surely that's been a problem since the beginning of time. Air...it's seldom thought about and taken for granted, but without it life does not exist. Unless something is very distinctive, we just don't notice it.*

I leaned my head against my hand. I was doing it now. I wasn't listening to the lecture... My mind was not there... My attention was not there... I was thinking about yesterday and tomorrow. *But why? Why do I think what's behind me and what's in front of me is more important than what is happening to me now? Why haven't I learned that today was tomorrow's yesterday?*

The longer I dwelled on it, the more I realized it made no sense.

Why do I feel what has already happened or that the next moment must be more important than the moment I am in? If I'm not careful I will miss my whole life, which is never not now. I'd heard it said, "You take care of tomorrow by taking care of today," and I believed it was Jesus who said, "Do not be anxious for tomorrow, for tomorrow will take care of itself." *Ugh, I really need to be an Oreo cookie — the stuff in the middle — the stuff in the middle is the now. That's the best part!*

My brain was whirling. *Yesterday is what happened, tomorrow is what will happen, but it is today, right now, that is happening. But what's happening? I don't know. This moment is happening and I need to be in it!*

The greatest gift that we as humans could give ourselves as well as another is our presence. *Our presence is the present. To live in the present moment may be considered a miracle because it releases the past, ignores the future, and only recognizes the moment. Living in the moment or being mindful of the moment requires a release of control. When we come to the end of our days, it is all about the moments — the memories of the events are all moments. Moments require our presence.*

"Mr. Brown... Mr. Brown? Earth to Mr. Brown!"

Jumping, I shook my head. "Yes, I'm sorry, sir?"

The professor arranged a few papers into his briefcase before heading toward the door. "Class is over, Mr. Brown. You may leave."

As if in a daze, I stood up from my desk, gathered my things, and trudged toward the door. I just missed about forty-five minutes of life because I was lost in the world between my ears and behind my eyes. There may have been some great moments that I didn't experience simply because I was not present.

I'm going to start right now in this moment living in the moment. Right now, while I'm walking, I'm going to focus on feeling my feet as they touch the ground. On the textures, the feelings, the overall sensation it gives my body. My new initiative is to be present in the present because...

*   *   *   *   *   *   *

Life occurs not in the days
but in the moments.

*   *   *   *   *   *   *

Hard Work

Week Forty-Nine

It had been a long, hot, humid summer. Untold pools of dried sweat had been seared into the cement driveway as Flo pushed through the heat to practice every single day. She performed drill after drill and shot every kind of shot imaginable over and over again. Ever since the school bell rang on the last day before summer vacation, Flo dedicated no less than an hour each day to improve her basketball skills. She was determined to finally make the high school varsity basketball team during her senior year.

Flo had started on the freshman team and then received solid minutes of play time her sophomore year on the junior varsity team. The next year, however, Flo had been upset when she discovered she'd been the last person cut during the Varsity tryouts. Basketball was one of her passions, and she couldn't put her finger on what had happened during those tryouts. She had spoken with the coach as soon as she'd seen the final cut list to inquire as to what she needed to do to make the team the next year. The coach gave her a few specific elements to work on, but gently reminded Flo that even if her skills improved she would still face the same stiff competition for a spot on the team next year and that the team was loaded with superior D-1 talent. Flo had trudged home in a fog of disappointment.

She sighed, allowing her thoughts to drift through memory lane.

Her entire family played basketball as she was growing up. Their games began in the house with nerf balls and a goal hooked to a door frame. Soon an adjustable goal stood in the driveway which moved up in height as Flo and her siblings grew. She had often thought as she dribbled up and down the driveway, *If I had a dollar for every time the basketball hit the concrete I would be a "gazillionaire!"* Like many others before her, young Flo had dreamed of playing before the big crowds, making the game winning shot, hearing the crowd's thunderous roar, having her picture on the Wheaties Box...all the contributing factors that drove a budding player to reach for the stars.

Flo enjoyed success in her early years hearing the crowds, albeit small, cheer her name as she was introduced or made a great play. During middle school, she made the winning shot from the field and from the free throw line in a battle against their rivals. Flo basked in the adulation, even if it was just eighth grade basketball; it felt great! One of Flo's distinguishing qualities was humility. She had a wonderful attitude on and off the court and did not allow her success to inflate her ego; she continued to walk through doors with plenty of room to spare on either side of her ears.

Naismith High was a perennial state powerhouse in girls' basketball and volleyball. Annually, Naismith High School graduated student athletes that went on to play in Division 1 basketball and volleyball programs. One of Flo's main goals was to play college basketball. She had even set her sights on a basketball scholarship to help her make that dream come true. When Flo entered high school, she hoped to make the Junior Varsity team. Somewhat disappointed but definitely not dissuaded, Flo made the 9th grade team instead of the JV team but had a solid freshman season.

She'd hoped that the JV coach had noticed her effort and skills in order to move up to the team once the freshman season was over. Only one ninth grader was moved up, but it was not Flo. Sheryl, Flo's best friend, had been selected for the JV team. Even though Flo was disappointed for herself, she was happy for Sheryl. They had grown up playing together and Flo could not deny the natural talent that Sheryl possessed. A basketball fit her like a hand fit a glove.

At the start of her sophomore year, Flo and Sheryl began meeting after school several days a week to prepare for the upcoming October tryouts. Flo was anxious. They pushed each other hard since they were both aiming to join the varsity team. The tryouts were tough, but all the work they put in had paid off, particularly in the suicide drills at the end of practice. The girls high fived each other at the end of each sequence of suicides, finishing in first and second place after each one.

The final cut list was posted; varsity and junior varsity team rosters were plastered outside the gym doors. Flo's heart skipped a beat when she did not see her name on the varsity roster...but there was Sheryl's. As her eyes continued to skim downward, she did receive some consolation in that she had made the junior varsity squad. Masking her disappointment was impossible. Her body language said it all.

Once again, Flo had a solid season. No longer was she one of the stars like in her earlier years, but she was a major contributor and a great team player. She was kind of like glue: not really noticed until needed. Even as a sophomore, Sheryl had been given significant playing time on the varsity squad and had diligently worked herself into the starting lineup by the end of the season. Flo regarded her friend with mixed emotions. She was happy for Sheryl, but frustrated that she didn't practice nearly as hard as Flo did and was still on the starting lineup for the varsity team.

Snapping herself back to the present, Flo was determined more than ever to rise to the challenge. She would not give up on her dream. She thought about the articles she had read over the years of the great athletes through history that overcame obstacles to achieve their goals to find success. Her thoughts wandered to Glen Cunningham who was considered America's greatest miler, even though when he was eight years old his legs were so severely burned that the medical community said he would never walk again. Then on to Michael Jordan, the greatest basketball player of all time, who was cut from his high school team when he was in the ninth grade. Finally, Satchell Paige, who realized his dream of pitching in the major leagues when he was forty-two years old.

You've got to believe to achieve, Flo thought to herself. She squared her shoulders and drew in a deep breath. *I can do this!*

Flo was excited about her senior year and felt at peace with the effort of her summer basketball practice, practice, practice! Even though she was anxious about the forthcoming basketball tryouts, she remained diligently focused on her academics. Her family loved athletics, but stressed an education. They always said, "Athletics can only carry you so far, but education can carry you all the way."

At last, it was October — time for tryouts! As she made her way to the sign-up sheet, Flo thought about how she tried to get Sheryl to come over and practice with her during the summer. Every once in a great while Sheryl would stop by when Flo was practicing, but it was token and very obvious that Sheryl had the "I'm good and don't need to practice" attitude. This had caused distance in their friendship, and it was evident to Flo that Sheryl thought her efforts were in vain. The team was set from last year; no one was leaving and there would not be room for Flo.

The tryouts were set for Monday, Tuesday, Wednesday, and Thursday. A cut list would be posted on the gym door the morning after each round of tryouts, resulting in the final team roster Friday morning. Monday's tryout was almost total conditioning, which was normal since its purpose was to weed out those who could not physically handle the exertion as well as to determine the truly dedicated athletes. Flo gave it everything she had. She tried not to follow the coaches' eyes to see if they were noticing her, but instead chose to focus her entire energy on each drill.

She felt good after Monday and was confident of her performance.

As soon as Flo arrived at school Tuesday, she made a bee-line for the gym, accompanied by the rest of the "non-returners." She was surprised that the returning players weren't scouring the list or even anywhere near the gym! They either knew something she didn't or they were mighty confident. Flo's finger zoomed down the list, freezing once it landed on her name. She nodded to herself with pride. *One down, three to go.*

Tuesday and Wednesday were full of skill drills and half court scrimmages. Flo held her own in both. Wednesday morning and Thursday morning found Flo's name on the list with two other non-returners. Thursday would be the big day; after warm ups the remaining time would be spent playing full court scrimmages.

Flo was focused. When she pushed through the gym doors for Thursday's tryout session, she was determined to leave it all on the floor— no prisoners, no excuses." Many times, Flo found herself either guarding or being guarded by Sheryl. Flo's hard work was apparent.

Sheryl seemed to be a day late and a dollar short each time she and Flo went head to head. On several occasions, from her peripheral vision, Flo noticed the coaches nodding and pointing her way before shifting her complete focus back to the scrimmage. Hope fluttered in her chest, but what she really wanted was for the head coach to take notice. He hadn't been at the tryouts since Monday!

Or so she thought.

Unbeknownst to the players, Coach Jackson was perched high above in the press box where no one could see him. He had decided to change his evaluation process this year because he noticed early on that some of his returning players had become complacent. He decided to observe without the chance of being noticed by the athletes. He wanted to see who was buying into his philosophy, which was repeated in unison before and after each practice, "practice like you play."

From his aerial view, Coach Jackson couldn't ignore Flo. It was obvious that she'd put in a lot of practice since last year's tryouts, and there was no denying that she wanted and was wholeheartedly fighting for a position on the team. He also remembered what he told Flo about superior talent, that all the players were returning, and basically hinting that she didn't stand a chance of making varsity.

Coach Jackson found that he had a lot to mull over before the final roster was posted.

Even though Flo was exhausted, physically and emotionally, she could not find sleep. She tossed and turned all Thursday night. When her alarm sounded the next morning, she groggily rolled out of bed to shower and get ready for school. Even though she sat down at the table for breakfast, the knot in her stomach was so large she couldn't eat and actually felt sick. She was a bundle of nerves, almost dreading going up to the gym doors to scour the final roster for her name.

As Flo prepared to leave the house, her father gave her a big hug. "Text me as soon as you can." Flo nodded against his shoulder before pulling back. He smiled down at her. "Did you do your best?" She nodded once more, to which he replied, "Then forget the rest."

It was a very long walk from the parking lot to the gym. The closer she got the harder her heart pounded in her chest. As Flo approached the gym there were already a bunch of girls searching for their names. Trinia, a non-returner, whipped around and away from the list with silent tears streaming down her cheeks. Flo's stomach dropped to the floor.

Trinia did a really great job! Blood rushed in Flo's ears as a new wave of anxiety washed over her. *Trinia definitely should have made the team!* Her breaths came in rapid puffs, and she was actually afraid she was going to start hyperventilating. *It's a good thing my lunch is in a paper bag.*

Once the group saw she had approached, everyone grew quiet. A shock of awareness shot down Flo's spine. *Oh no! This is a bad sign.* She swallowed hard against the nausea building in her stomach all the while avoiding eye contact with the girls staring at her. *Brace yourself!*

Biting her lower lip, she very slowly eyed the roster. Starting from the top she read the names, deliberately in slow motion, as she worked down the page. Her heart sank lower and lower, until she found herself staring at the very last name... Her head felt light... Her knees buckled... A huge grin spread across her face...

Florence Johnson.

She did it! She'd made the team! Elated, she took a deep breath to gather her composure just in time to notice that Sheryl stood beside her in stupefied shock. The name *Sheryl Robertson* could be found nowhere on the list. With trembling hands, Florence pulled her phone from her pocket to text a message to her father. *I made it, Dad! I actually made it! And Sheryl didn't – can you believe it?!*

She received an instantaneous reply that put the icing on her cake. He replied, "Always remember that...

* * * * * * *

Hard work beats talent when talent doesn't work hard.

* * * * * * *

Graffiti

Week Fifty

"It's so good to see all of you today; I see so many familiar faces and it appears as if some of you have brought friends along. For those of you that have never been to one of my conferences, I am Guru Garysheema, a lifelong student of life. It is my desire to challenge the paradigms each of you have constructed thus far within your life's journey. It is not my intent to provide answers, but rather to pose questions meant to help each of you discover an answer unique to you and your journey." He smiled before adding, "Please note, I said *an answer not the answer.* Well, my friends, let us begin."

As I gazed around the room, I saw a lot of familiar faces seated in the crowd. *That Guru Garysheema is all right by me,* I thought to myself in eager anticipation. *I feel like a groupie; I attend all his lectures and seminars. He just has a way of presenting thought-provoking concepts in such a nonthreatening manner, and it actually allows individuals to decide what they will do with it and how they can incorporate it within their own lives. I'm surprised the guru has been able to fly under the radar and not get caught up in all of the hype of the New Age movement. Obviously, he's comfortable in his skin and enjoys his low key traveling "tent revival" type of teaching style. I find his style so refreshing in such a fast-paced, high-maintenance world.*

"Today, my friends, we will talk about mistakes," the guru said as he stood up from his cross-legged position. "So, what is a mistake?" He paused briefly before answering his own question. "By definition, it is 'to make an incorrect choice, known or unknown, to misunderstand the meaning or intention, to make an incorrect judgment, to identify incorrectly.' A mistake can take many forms and can create decisions with outcomes, positive and negative. A mistake can create all types of emotions, positive and negative. A mistake means imperfection. Of course, the knowledge of that imperfection is typically discovered in hindsight."

"Tell me," he continued, "isn't the family we are born into imperfect? Isn't the world we live within imperfect? Are you perfect? I will answer for you, *no.* Do you want to be perfect? I surely hope not."

Guru Garysheema clasped his hands together. "You say, *hold on, I actually do want to be perfect.* To that, I say what good would the experience of life be if you were perfect and knew all the right answers and all of the outcomes? What good comes out of being right all the time? Is it just so you can tell others, *I told you so?* What would be the point of living, of experiencing, of learning, of growing if you were perfect?"

Wow, that's really interesting. I do know I like being right, but I am grasping what the guru is saying. Glancing around quickly, it was obvious that everyone was pondering the guru's words based on the myriad of expressions plastered on their faces.

"Instead of pursuing perfection why not embrace imperfection? *Learn* from it. *Discover* who you really are. *Embrace* the fact that everything is flawed and through those flaws wisdom is discovered. As humbling as our mistakes might be, it is ultimately the *wrong,* not the *right,* that can teach us who we really are. Wisdom is the ability to make the right choices, and this ability is many times developed by the consequences of making the wrong choices...making mistakes. When we realize imperfection is in *all,* it allows us to resign as king or queen of the universe. It actually takes a lot of pressure off of us to allow ourselves to be imperfect in our daily lives. Does that mean you are intentionally trying to make mistakes, that you have no regard for the highest and best, or that you do not care about excellence? No, of course not. It simply means when a mistake has been made, you *acknowledge* it, *accept* the consequences of it, *learn* from it, then *carry the lesson forward.*"

"Everyone, please stand." The guru paused patiently as we followed his initial direction. "Now, inhale and stretch your arms upward. Stretch to the sky above on your tiptoes. Hold that stretch.

And exhale and release the stretch. Very good. Please be seated." As he waited for us to settle back into our chairs, he gazed around the room with a smile.

"Reach under your seats. You will each find a drawing pad and piece of charcoal." The guru motioned for an associate to come on to the stage. She walked up carrying a large vase overflowing with a beautiful bouquet of flowers. Within the vibrant collage, I immediately recognized zinnias, gladiolas, gerbera daisies, and snapdragons that were beautifully arranged.

The associate gently placed the vase of flowers beside the guru and left the stage. Guru Garysheema nodded his thanks before speaking to us once more. "Please, take a moment to study this beautiful bouquet, then use the drawing pad and charcoal to sketch what you see. We will spend about thirty minutes drawing, and as you work I will be walking around the room to view your artwork." The guru chuckled in understanding when a few members of the crowd gawked at him in horror. "Yes, yes, I know all of us are not artists, but the point of this exercise is for you to draw to the best of *your* ability what you see here on the stage. Please begin."

I frowned at the flowers. *I am definitely one of those "stick figure artists," so this will be quite a challenge for me.* It wasn't long before I made an errant stroke. *Okay, I need to erase...um, uh-oh...there's no eraser under the chair.* Peeking over my shoulder, I could see several other people rummaging under their seats. They must have made a mistake, too. *All right, no eraser, no big deal. Let me try to rub the mark away.* I cringed. *Great, now I have a big smudge. Well, let me see what I can do. Oh man, another bad stroke. I can't erase it and if I try to rub with my finger it just makes it worse. Eh, let me just try to work around it.*

For the next thirty minutes, all that could be heard was the sound of charcoal sliding over paper mingled with intermittent groans and grunts. Guru Garysheema weaved in and out of the rows where we worked tirelessly the entire time, smiling, nodding, and taking it all in.

As he stepped back on to the stage, the guru said, "Everyone, let us put down our charcoal and stop drawing." He gave close to a minute's time for each participant to finish up the last strokes of their drawing before continuing with his directions. "Please, stand and stretch with your hands to the sky up high on your toes. And release. Now, please take your drawing and set it in your seat. We will spend the next ten minutes walking around the room to view each other's renderings."

Several of the drawings I gazed down at were outstanding. One, in fact, appeared to be so life like, I was tempted to touch the charcoal petals that seemed to jump off the page. However, most were like mine, well intentioned, but fraught with errant lines, smudges, and extraterrestrial flowers. Once we had maneuvered through most of the rows within the room, the guru asked that we return to our seats.

"Today, we learned what it is like to depict life on canvas. Each of you drew to the best of your ability. Many of you drew lines and images that you were not pleased with and you tried to change. You were disheartened when you discovered you were not provided with an eraser. That is just like our waking life. We talk, hear, see, act, react, interact each and every day, but we cannot take any of it, the good or the bad, back. We cannot erase it. Yes, sometimes we try to cover it up, but it is still there; maybe not seen today, but surely tomorrow or tomorrow's tomorrow."

He paused thoughtfully before continuing. "Recently, I heard a great street artist define his approach to graffiti. He said, 'Never erase; fix it, make it work, make it fit in.' I have pondered over his statement. That is what we have to do in life. We all make mistakes. We cannot take them back. We cannot rewrite history. We can make believe mistakes do not exist, but they do. Instead we should *embrace* our mistakes, *admit* our mistakes, and most importantly learn from our mistakes. It is in doing this that we discover who we truly are and that we have the power to change our lives for the better and grow into wiser individuals by utilizing the lessons learned from our past mistakes. In life, just like with your drawing, we should remember...

*   *   *   *   *   *   *

Don't erase.

Just move forward and incorporate

your mistakes

into the masterpiece of your life.

*   *   *   *   *   *   *

*   *   *   *   *   *   *

Reindeer

*   *   *   *   *   *   *

Week Fifty-One

"Okay, everyone," Santa began at the annual "After Christmas" debriefing, "another really great Christmas season. A job well done to everyone!" A round of applause sounded throughout the Great Hall. After a few moments of cheer, Santa held up his hand to silence the crowd and turned his attention to the reindeer. "I've been thinking, and next year I want your boys to pull the sleigh. It's time to put those young fellas to work and see what they're made of."

A murmur of exclamation, confusion, and shock ran rampant through the group of reindeer, which reached all the way back to the elves, who immediately huddled together to discuss in hushed voices the unexpected announcement.

"The big question is," Santa continued, stroking his long, white beard in pontification, "who will lead the team? Will it be your son, Dasher? Or yours, Dancer? What about yours, Prancer, Vixen, Comet? Or yours, Cupid, Donner, Blitzen? Which one will it be? Will it be Frank, Jose, Pete, Wong, Bert, Tom, Jermaine, or Rudolph?"

Santa paused as the reindeer exploded with declarations of whose son should receive the honor of leading the sleigh. The elves buried themselves deeper into their huddle. Santa held up his hand once more and a hush fell over the reindeer.

"We have an entire year for one of your boys to prove that he has what it takes to lead our team. We will also be flying in a new formation... more of a triangular fashion instead of a rectangular one. I have been thinking the 'one, two, two, three' formation will be more wind dynamic, allowing us to cover more ground in less amount of time. That means, of course, the lead will have an extremely important responsibility for the well-being of the team as well as Christmas itself."

The reindeer were silent.

Santa clapped his hands. "Meeting adjourned everyone! Enjoy a much deserved break!" He turned to the reindeer once more. "When you all get home, be sure and tell your sons what we've discussed. And tell them that Mrs. Claus and I will be watching."

North Pole was soon abuzz, as Santa's grand plan for the next Christmas Eve's run was the hot topic of conversation. All the elves in the workshop argued who they believed would become the next lead deer. Bernard, the senior elf supervisor, even set up odds and began taking bets.

Throughout the year, the young stags did everything they could to gain Santa's favor. Whatever Santa said, they agreed with. Whatever Santa wanted, they fell over themselves and each other trying to get it. They washed his windows, polished the sleigh, cleaned his house, took out the garbage, offered a handkerchief every time Santa even thought about sneezing, decked his halls, trimmed his trees, and brought his groceries home from the store. You name it, they did it.

"I will be so glad when you announce your decision," Mrs. Claus told Santa one night, "because, I swear, it has gotten to the place that if you open your mouth too wide there are reindeer eyes staring back at me." Santa only laughed, although he knew it was true.

As the months continued, the young reindeer continued to be at Santa's beck and call. Well, all except for Rudolph. Some of the elves noticed that Rudolph was not playing the "reindeer games," as it had come to be called around the North Pole. Rudolph was less concerned with being noticed and more concerned with quietly completing acts of service he noticed in and around the North Pole. If he saw something needed to be done or someone needed help, he did it all in stride, expecting nothing in return.

"Dude," Bernard advised Rudolph one afternoon, "you better get with it, or you're going to be on the back row pulling that sled. Believe it or not, I have a bunch of money riding on you."

Rudolph grinned. "My father always says 'be yourself, be an original,' which I have really taken to heart since I have this red nose to deal with. I have just decided it's better for me to continue to be myself and to not get caught up in the chase to the top of the sleigh."

After almost three hundred and forty days of "Santa butt kissing" from seven upstarts all trying to make a name for themselves, Santa was finally ready to announce his decision. At the "Celebration of the Christmas Season" festival held annually on the first day of December, Santa began by chuckling.

"Well, it has been a very interesting year, wouldn't you all say?" A rumble of agreement rambled through the crowd. "I had no idea when I made the announcement last year that I would witness such energy," he paused before suddenly frowning and shaking his head, "such hoofing on one another, such antler tooting, and such patronizing behavior."

He gazed down at the young reindeer before him. The heads, only seconds before held high, dropped down towards the ground. All except Rudolph's. Santa's eyes shifted to land on him.

"After much deliberation, observation, and thought, I have decided that the lead deer for this year's Christmas Eve will be none other than...RUDOLPH!"

A gasp sounded from the group of reindeer while the elves burst into cheer.

"What?!" exclaimed Frank.

"Unbelievable!" cried Jose.

"Unreal," muttered Pete angrily.

"You have got to be kidding me," Wong retorted with an eye roll.

"After all I did?!" blurted out Bert.

"After all you did?" Tom argued. "How about after all we did?!"

"Wow, man!" Jermaine shook his head in disbelief.

Santa silenced the crowd. He turned to the angry reindeer. "In order to be on a team such as this, you must work together instead of fighting against each other. You must build each other up instead of putting each other down. You must lead by example and not be afraid that others may not follow you instead of jumping on the bandwagon. Rudolph has shown these qualities through acts of selfless service. He has proven himself this year to be the most capable of leading the sleigh."

Rudolph smiled graciously and bowed his head toward Santa. At the end of the hall, Bernard could be heard telling all the elves, "Pay up, pay up," because...

*   *   *   *   *   *   *

Santa's favorite reindeer has a <u>red</u> nose and is not a <u>brown</u> nose.

*   *   *   *   *   *   *

*   *   *   *   *   *   *

Hurdles

*   *   *   *   *   *   *

Week Fifty-Two

We are all still dressed in our warmups, waiting anxiously for the start of the 110-meter high hurdle finals. I had been preparing for this day for years. My chest tightens. Years of hard work, sweat, disappointment, perseverance, elation, wins, losses, sacrifices, medals, and trophies will culminate in just a few minutes in the world's greatest international competition: The Olympics.

I am representing my country with a chance to stand on that podium...thousands and thousands of eyes are glued to me...not just in the stadium, but all across the world. It is simply unbelievable. There is no denying I'm nervous. My heart is pounding. Blood roars in my ears. My very limbs seem to pulse with an abundance of adrenaline...but I have to focus.

I shake my head side to side. My arms fly in large circles to warm up through windmills. My core elongates and tightens with trunk rotations. After shaking out each leg, I perform a series of lower body stretches that focus on the hamstrings, calves, and groin muscles. Truly, I would have performed any movement that sprang to my mind, anything to occupy myself from the incessant nerves spreading through my body. Personally, if I focus too much on the race in front of me, by the time my feet position themselves into the starting blocks, I am practically out of breath. I certainly cannot chance that happening during this, the most important race of my life.

The PA system blares, "Five minutes! Five minutes! The 110-meter high hurdles begins in five minutes!"

The stadium is abuzz with anticipation. Each of us competing in the race strip off our sweat suits and take warm up starts from the blocks of our assigned lanes. The adrenaline is flowing and we are all nervous. The energy is alive and can be felt and can also be seen shining in our eyes...even though most of us are unwilling to make eye contact with each other because of how high the stakes are.

My father's sound advice, given to me when I first began racing, rings clearly in my ears. "Being nervous is natural. Use it to your advantage. Draw on that energy to push you faster."

The PA system blares again. "Runners, please make your way to the starting blocks for the 110-meter high hurdles! Runners, please make your way to the starting blocks for the 110-meter high hurdles!"

We apprehensively head to our assigned lanes. The stadium hushes to a tense quiet. All eyes are on us.

My heart thumps forcefully against my chest, desperate to burst free. Sweat, cold and clammy, beads along my forehead and upper lip. *Breathe,* I reassure myself. *Breathe, slow down, smile, and relax. This is what you have been training for. This is your moment.*

"Runners, take your marks!"

Our feet set in our respective starting blocks as we place our hands so our fingers barely graze the starting line in an attempt to try and gain any possible advantage. Our bodies tense in preparation to bolt out of the blocks to fly down the track. The start is always the key to success.

The stadium is still...silent, eerily so, given the fact that over fifty thousand people of all ages are now quiet at the exact same time.

"Set!"

My gaze, mind, and body are focused solely on the track.

POP! Just as the starter's pistol is fired, deafening roars of applause and cheers erupt from the stadium as anticipation and execution intersect while we fly forward from the starting blocks.

"It's a fair start!"

Breathing steadily, I am in full stride, just like all the runners, and am halfway to the first hurdle. Prepping myself for the leap, I smoothly clear the first hurdle without a hitch. Feeling good, I know that I am in my element. It is like the wind is at my back, pushing me, lifting me, guiding me, as I glide down the track. Focused with eyes straight ahead, all I see are the hurdles in front of me...but I'm not detecting any other body movement in my peripheral vision. *Odd. I must be making great time! I know this is going to be a P.B. - personal best! I am going to win this. Go man, go man, go!*

Clearing the second hurdle in full stride with several inches to spare between the hurdle and my body, I am defying gravity! I am close to flying, and I know without a doubt there is a large "S" plastered on my chest. *But where are all the other runners?*

Unable to quell my curiosity, I peek over my left shoulder to see...no one? *Huh?* Glancing over my right shoulder I see...nobody? *What the –*

In less than the blink of an eye, a hurdle is on top of me! Scrambling to regain focus, I graze the top, landing with a slight buckle that causes me to barely break stride. Eyes darting side to side, I, surprisingly, don't see *anyone.* Forcing myself to concentrate, my foot actually plants itself directly in the middle of the hurdle, causing me to bring it crashing to the ground with my lead foot. I am surveying the competition as soon as my foot hits the ground, and I still see...*no one!*

My performance must be better than what I think, I convince myself. With sweat streaking down my face, I can physically feel my form crumbling...and hurdling is all about form.

On the next hurdle, I sail in the air, clearing it with my lead foot, but, *ouch,* clipping it with my rear. *Wow,* I breath through the pain, *that hurt! That will be black and blue tomorrow. But no one has caught me! Keep fighting! You're getting close and there is no one near you.*

Lifting to prepare for the next hurdle, I instantly know my form is completely off. *This is not going to be good.* I clip the hurdle with my front foot, followed by my back knee, and stumble. As I am flailing about, knowing I resemble a chicken running around aimlessly with its head cut off, I'm amazed that no one has passed me.

Regaining my balance, I instinctively prepare for the next obstacle only to suddenly experience every hurdler's nightmare: a fall.

Whap!

When I hit the ground in a face plant, my hopes and dreams seemingly evaporate before my eyes. *Get up!* I order myself in desperation. Painstakingly clamoring to my feet to resume running, I abruptly realize with a shock that I am alone.

There are no other runners.

What is going on? It's just me out here! I'm alone on the track! My legs slow until my feet plow along at a hobbling jog. Approaching the last hurdle, I gingerly leap and then cross the finish line. There is nothing but silence to greet me.

The stands are empty. *What just happened?* I turn a slow circle. Not a soul can be seen.

What is going on?

My eyes snap open. I am foggy and groggy. As I blink to take in the familiar sights of my bedroom, I sigh a breath of relief. *A dream. Wow. Just a dream. But so real.* I peel the damp sheets away from my clammy skin while my heart continues to thunder in my chest, all the while pondering this dream and its meaning.

*   *   *   *   *   *   *

Life is like a track and all of us face daily hurdles. Success depends on how we accept all the many challenges that come our way, not just the ones we can easily hurdle. We must use the hurdles of life as stepping stones even when they may at first be stumbling blocks. We must strive each day to live better, stronger, and truer lives. We must press on like the hurdler in the race. We must master some weakness and repair mistakes. We must choose to focus on our own challenges without focusing on the positions of others in the race. Surpass yesterday, if not today, then tomorrow. We must have a vision larger than the obstacle before us. We must complete the race and cross the finish line. More than anything we must realize...

*　*　*　*　*　*　*

Life is not so much a competition

with <u>others</u>

but more with <u>ourself</u> .

*　*　*　*　*　*　*

www.ingramcontent.com/pod-product-compliance
Lightning Source LLC
Chambersburg PA
CBHW032103280326
41933CB00009B/748